DATE DUE

92
Ha

Robbins, Neal E.

Rutherford B. Hayes,
19th president

GUMDROP BOOKS - Bethany, Missouri

Rutherford B. Hayes

19th President of the United States

Rutherford B. Hayes rose to the presidency on the strength of his fame as a war hero and record in public office. He served a single, stormy term that ushered in reforms of the federal government and eased post-Civil War tensions between North and South. (Library of Congress.)

Rutherford B. Hayes

19th President of the United States

Neal E. Robbins

 GARRETT EDUCATIONAL CORPORATION

Cover: *Official presidential portrait of Rutherford B. Hayes by Daniel Huntington.* (Copyrighted by the White House Historical Association; photograph by the National Geographic Society.)

Manufactured in the United States of America

Edited and produced by Synthegraphics Corporation

Library of Congress Cataloging in Publication Data

Robbins, Neal E., 1954–
  Rutherford B. Hayes, 19th president of the United States.
  (Presidents of the United States)
  Bibliography: p.
  Includes index.
  Summary: Follows the life of Rutherford B. Hayes, including his childhood, education, employment, political career, and term of presidency.
  1. Hayes, Rutherford Birchard, 1822–1893 – Juvenile literature. 2. Presidents – United States – Biography – Juvenile literature. 3. Hayes, Rutherford Birchard, 1822–1893 – Juvenile literature. I. Title. II. Title: Rutherford B. Hayes, nineteenth president of the United States. III. Series.
  [DNLM: 1. Presidents.]
E682.R6 1989   973.8′3′0924 – dc19   [B]   [92]
88-24565
ISBN 0-944483-23-2

Contents

Chronology for Rutherford B. Hayes

1822   Born on October 4 in Delaware, Ohio

1838–
1842   Attended Kenyon College

1843–
1845   Attended Harvard Law School

1852   Married Lucy Ware Webb on December 30

1858–
1861   Served as city solicitor of Cincinnati

1861–
1865   Served in 23rd Ohio Volunteer Regiment; rose to rank of brevet major general

1865–
1867   Served in the U.S. House of Representatives

1868–
1872   Served as governor of Ohio for two terms

1876–
1877   Served a third term as governor of Ohio

1877–
1881   Served as 19th President of the United States after Congress had to settle a disputed election

1889   Wife died on June 25

1893   Died on January 17 in Fremont, Ohio

Chapter 1

Beloved Son

In a rhythm of long and short clicks, electrical impulses surged out of the telegraph, sending 10 words to the men waiting at St. Mary's Station in Harrisburg, Pennsylvania. The telegram from Washington was raced to a train waiting in the darkness outside. Bearers carried it to the berth of Rutherford B. Hayes, who lay asleep next to his wife. They awakened him and watched at his bedside as he read: "BOTH HOUSES ADJOURNED. HAYES DULY DECLARED ELECTED. GLORY TO GOD."

A months-long dispute over who won the presidential election of November 7, 1876, had been resolved! Only on receiving this message on March 2, 1877, two days before a legal deadline, did Hayes know for sure he would be President. The time for celebration had arrived at last.

The news of the triumph by the Ohio Republican reached him in Harrisburg while he was already on his way to Washington to claim the prize. The little knot of supporters gathered around the President-elect began to cheer noisily. But Hayes, still in his bed clothes, looked pale and serious. "Boys, boys, boys," he cried, "don't make so much noise—it will waken the passengers."

In silencing the celebrators, who quietly returned to their train cars, Hayes revealed more than a courteous nature. His actions suggested that his feelings about the victory were tinged with anxiety.

Hayes had good reason to be uneasy. The election had been the most extraordinary presidential contest in American history. It was an election marred by massive cheating and behind-the-scenes deals. Both sides engaged in trickery, but the Democrats became so angry when defeat loomed that many vowed to take up arms if Hayes won. Their threats terrified a nation with still-fresh memories of the Civil War and the murder of President Abraham Lincoln.

The losers believed, perhaps rightly, that the voters had really elected their candidate, Samuel J. Tilden. The electoral college, however, could not decide on a winner. The dispute was then taken to Congress, which haggled and delayed but finally decided in Hayes' favor. Tilden, wishing to avoid violence, refused to fight the judgment, which most Democrats never accepted. Doubts did not die, and bitterness dogged Hayes' single, stormy term as President.

But now, Rutherford B. Hayes held in his hands the telegram marking the end of that long, tiring election. He could put the conflict behind him and turn to the challenges ahead. He would have to fight for his rights as President, fend off political bosses who made claims on his powers, and deal with a prickly Congress. He would also have to defuse unresolved tensions between the North and South simmering since the Civil War, more than a decade before. But there, on the train, these hurdles must have seemed distant. Despite the recent past, Hayes could momentarily savor victory—the presidency was his.

A FATHERLESS BOY

On October 4, 1822, in the town of Delaware, Ohio, a feverish Sophia Hayes was about to give birth. Her brother Sardis rushed out to get a doctor. He returned to the red brick house on Williams Street with Dr. Lamb and his nurse. They attended to the weakened mother, delivering a boy at around nine o'clock that night. Sardis lit a fire in the house to ward off the evening chill and paid the good doctor $3.50 for his services.

The child, to be baptized the following spring as Rutherford Birchard Hayes, was thin and sickly. Many doubted he would survive. Neighbors who came around to visit made bleak predictions. "He [will] die," said one, "and it is a waste of strength. I tell you the child is not worth saving." People got in the habit of asking if Mrs. Hayes' baby had died the night before.

For the first two years, Sophia worried about Rutherford's survival. His weakness and the deaths of two of her earlier children filled her with dread. Adding to her fears was the fact that just 10 weeks before Rutherford's birth, his father, Ruddy, had died of fever. Giving birth in the depths of almost unbearable grief, Sophia seemed to find strength in the needs of the tiny infant. She dedicated herself to him, sheltering the boy from harm and showering him with motherly attention.

One of the boarders Sophia took in to help support the family made light of her concerns over Rutherford. "In a year or two he will be all head," joked Sam Rheem, a mason and lifelong family friend. "Stick to him! I shouldn't wonder if he should really come to something yet."

Until he was seven, the blue-eyed, reddish-brown-haired boy nicknamed "Rud" was not allowed to play with children outside the family. He was nine before he could even take part in sports. He just stayed home, where he had the love of his mother and of Sophia's cousin, Arcena Smith; his uncle, Sardis Birchard; his sister Fanny; and, briefly, that of brother Lorenzo. When Rud was two years old, Lorenzo, age nine, drowned in an ice-skating accident at a millpond.

Sophia's suffering over Lorenzo's death redoubled her determination to nurture and protect her younger son. Though Rud was too small to remember Lorenzo, his brother would become a family hero along with his father. The family's bright recollections of Ruddy's energy and drive, and of Lorenzo's kindness and courage, would represent a tall standard against which Rud would measure himself.

A World at Home

In 1817, four years after Rud's father, Rutherford "Ruddy" Hayes, and Sophia had married in Vermont, they loaded the family into covered wagons and headed west. The 40-day trip in search of greater prosperity brought them to Ohio, then still part of the western frontier. When Ruddy died, Sophia took charge, supporting the family on rents from lodgers and income from the farm she owned outside town.

Sophia was a strict Presbyterian who loved to talk about religion and politics. She would engage wandering ministers in long discussions of the latest ideas about God and Christianity. The family would often talk about problems concerning government, slavery, and politics in Washington. Oddly, however, she hated the idea of Rud ever becoming a politician because of what had happened to her brother-in-law, John Noyes, when he was a congressman from Vermont. He had ended his term as an alcoholic, declaring, "It's a dog's life — and worse!"

Having no father, little Rud sought fathering from the men of the house. He looked mainly to Uncle Sardis, a self-educated, hard-drinking frontiersman. Rud wanted to be just like Sardis, who returned the affection and would become Rud's lifelong patron.

Rud's house was on a corner lot, well shaded by large locust trees. At the side, the children used an ample grass lot as a playground. There was a small orchard of apple, peach, quince, and cherry trees there. Currant bushes grew in abundance. Rud and his sister Fanny, two years his senior, played in the yard on warm days. They lay in the shade of the big cherry tree, curling dandelion stems and hanging them from their ears or digging little wells in the mud. On other days, they played inside as light shining through the curtained glass windows illuminated the whitewashed rooms. Fanny would read to him from her books and invent games, or they would turn a poem like *Lady of the Lake* into a little play.

Rud admired Fanny. A precocious child, she had read all of Shakespeare's plays by age 12. She was Rud's constant childhood companion, but sometimes they squabbled, mostly when Fanny teased him. "How I feared her ridicule," he would later recall.

Rud looked up to Fanny as his "protector and nurse." Later, he would call her his "dear one" and his inspiration. She, even more than Sardis or Sophia, urged Rud to work to become "somebody important." She believed in him and identified with him. She so shared his dreams that he grew up anxious to fulfill her expectations.

YOUNG DREAMER

Rud stood out among other boys his age for his dreams, his self-confidence, and his steadfastness. From childhood he began keeping a diary that he would write in throughout his life. When older, he would remember himself as a boy who "was always ambitious, dreaming of future glory, of performing some virtuous or patriotic action," especially "of military fame." He loved to play orator, and a young cousin was so impressed with his cleverness that she was sure he would one day be President of the United States. He said of himself that

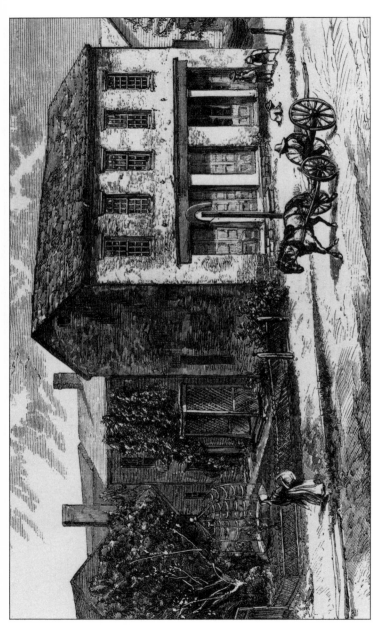

This house in Delaware, Ohio, was built for the family by Rutherford "Rud" Hayes' father, who died just before Rud was born there. Rud later wrote fondly about his upbringing in the home, particularly of playing in the shaded yard with his sister, Fanny. (Library of Congress.)

he was "remarkable for self-esteem," but also confessed at times to be "nervous to the verge of disaster." He "went to pieces on the slightest provocation." Rud ascribed his nervousness to a fear of insanity in his family.

From Pupil to Scholar

Rud began his formal education at a private school in Delaware, Ohio. He then attended Norwalk Academy, a Methodist boarding school in Norwalk, Ohio. Uncle Sardis often visited Rud at Norwalk, writing reassuringly to his worried mother that the institution would not corrupt her 14-year-old's morals. This was a constant concern for Sophia, who fretted over Rud's loud voice and "unpolished manners." She wanted him to be a gentleman.

After a year at Norwalk, Sardis got Rud into Isaac Webb's Preparatory School in Middletown, Connecticut. Then, in 1838, he was enrolled in Kenyon College, at Gambier, Ohio, where he studied the Greek and Latin classics, Christian ethics, theology, and other subjects considered necessary for a cultivated and educated man of the time.

Reverend Dr. Sparrow, the head of Kenyon, maintained rigid discipline at the institution. But that did not prevent Rud from indulging in forbidden fun, such as hunting. He also resisted his teachers' efforts to win his declaration of faith to Christianity. "There are now but ten in the whole college who are not changed," he wrote to his mother. "I am among the ten as yet. . . . Every single one of my best friends is 'gone.'" This, no doubt, was not what Sophia wanted to hear. She was already upset when, on returning home one vacation, Rud used a vulgar phrase he picked up at college. "I never heard you say 'By George' till the last time you were home, nor speak any other such language!" she remarked in a letter.

Rud's correspondence with Fanny often focused on his

school work. She was ever urging him on. "Be a good boy. Be first in your class. Keep your teeth clean. Nails ditto. . . . " she wrote. "Do not waste your time at school as so many do. You *must* turn out a genius." But despite his sister's pressure, Rud did not work especially hard at first.

Attitude Toward Slavery

Rud wanted to be a lawyer. He showed his desire for law by helping to settle arguments over slavery that would break out between northern and southern students at Kenyon. Though the Civil War was still over 20 years in the future, the issue of slavery divided students, sometimes sparking fist fights. Rud stepped in a number of times to help ease tensions. "Treat the Southerners as at least fellow countrymen and do unto them as they would do unto us, if we were in their situation," Rud told his fellow students. He came to be known as "the levelest head in the college."

Rud could play the role of "mediator"—one who helps settle arguments—in part because he was a good talker. His early fondness for oratory stayed with him at Kenyon, where he participated in debating tournaments that involved the issue of slavery. But as a young man, he did not have strong feelings about the subject. Later, however, he would one day fight to abolish slavery.

Rud's attitude toward slavery was not surprising. His family favored the practical, moderate, but morally lukewarm views of the Whig Party—the political party of stability. Sardis (who had once run unsuccessfully for state office as a Whig) and Sophia frowned on slavery on moral grounds. But like many northerners, they strongly opposed the abolitionists—those who wanted to do away with or abolish slavery. Abolitionism threatened the harmony of North and South and went against the basic law of the nation, the Constitution, which had left the question of slavery up to the individual states.

At Kenyon, many faculty members, including President Sparrow, defended the practice of slavery, and Rud did not have much reason to think differently. The only direct experience he had with slavery came from discussions with well-to-do southern classmates like Texan Guy M. Bryan, an honorable southern gentleman and Rud's distant cousin. These conversations tended to moderate Rud's views of slavery and of southerners for years to come.

A Changed Student

Rud became a serious college student only after the marriage of his sister, Fanny. When Fanny wrote to Rud at Kenyon to tell him that she would soon be marrying businessman William Augustus Platt, she also said that Rud should "try to like him well enough for a brother." But because Rud had always been so close to his sister, he found it difficult to accept the fact that there would now be another man in her life who would be just as important to her as he had been.

In a letter to Fanny conveying his congratulations, Rud could not bring himself to use the words "married" or "husband." He used dashes instead. He also could not bring himself to attend her wedding in Columbus, Ohio, on September 2, 1839. However, after finally accepting his sister's marriage, Rud realized that he had his own life to live. It was then that he became a hard-working, diligent student.

Chapter 2

High Expectations

One day in April 1842, a letter arrived from Rud's brother-in-law, Will Platt. Rud had just returned from a visit to the Platts' home in Columbus, during which Fanny gave birth to her second child. Upon opening the letter he read that since the night of his departure, Fanny had become "mentally deranged." She had become so violent that she had to be tied to her bed. Rud later learned that during the first days of her illness, Fanny had inquired about him continually. She would not believe he had left.

Within days, the family had committed Fanny to an asylum, an institution for mentally disturbed people. "This may startle you, my dear brother, and pierce your soul, but severe as it is you must know the truth," is how Will told Rud of Fanny's condition. Rud was shattered. He could not bear to visit Fanny in the asylum.

In August of 1842 Rud graduated from Kenyon. Only Sardis and his mother attended the ceremony. He had finished top in his class of nine students, earning the honor of giving the valedictory address. Looking quite impressive in his graduation clothes, the slim 20-year-old gave a speech on "College Life." He said that any future "respectability and influence" class members attained would remind them of the teachers "who fixed our fortunes by molding our minds in youth."

Fortunately, by autumn Fanny had completely recovered from her illness, and Rud went to live with her and Will in Columbus. It was now the home of his mother, too, who had moved in with Fanny after selling the house in Delaware. In the Platts' ample home, the family found pleasant togetherness.

Rud set to work preparing himself to be a lawyer. He studied at the office of a local law firm, which is how most lawyers were trained in those days. But he soon wanted better teachers, so he decided to attend Harvard Law School. Uncle Sardis gladly paid the tuition. "The money will be well paid out," he declared. "Rutherford is a sound boy and has got good sense, like a horse."

"MEND! MEND!"

Cambridge [Massachusetts], August 28, 1843 – The term commences today. Whatever resolution and ability I have shall now be brought out. I have much lost time to regain and my mind to discipline.

So resolved the young "R. B. Hayes," as he then signed his letters. After a few months of hard study he reported that "Law School satisfies me well." He pushed himself to perform, but part of him was never satisfied. "Oh, how little have I done! How little have I learned!" was a typical remark as he plowed through classical literature, philosophy, French, German, Latin, Greek, and law.

Great thinkers would lecture at the school, including the orator Daniel Webster, the poet Henry Wadsworth Longfellow, and former President John Quincy Adams. Rud often mulled over the various ideas he heard, weighing religious, legal or political views against one another, but he rarely came to a firm conclusion. Typical was the debate over slavery, which at Harvard also led to student brawls. He listened with interest to Adams speaking for an end to slavery. But Law Professor Joseph Story, a Supreme Court justice who defended the constitutional rights of slaveowners, left just as big an impression.

As he grew intellectually, Rud became more aware of the need to grow to manhood. "Trifling remarks, boyish conduct are my angry sins. Mend! Mend!" he chastised himself. Near the end of his three 20-week terms at Harvard, he proclaimed that he must strive to be "in manners, morals and feelings a true gentleman." With this resolution, on January 17, 1845, he was graduated with a bachelor of laws degree. "Now I shall begin to *live!*" he wrote in his diary.

RISING STAR OF OHIO

After passing the bar examination at Marietta, Ohio, on March 10, 1845, Rud chose to begin his law career in Lower Sandusky, Ohio. His mother and sister had wanted him near them in Columbus, the state capital, where he would enjoy the "opportunity to see legal procedures conducted in the largest scale." The advantages of being in the state capital, however, would put him too close to home. Moreover, as a young lawyer concerned about his success, he knew that it was easier to start out in a small town. Lower Sandusky was also the home of Uncle Sardis, who was ready to help Rutherford along in any way he could.

R. B. Hayes, Esq., put out his lawyer's shingle on a dusty street in the town. There, in a little room about 15 feet square, clients presented the young attorney with their weighty legal problems: disputes over land titles, divorces, and the drawing up of wills.

R.B. Hayes, Esq., as a young lawyer at 24 years of age. He stayed clean-shaven until becoming a soldier in the Civil War. (Library of Congress.)

At day's end, Rutherford would return to his room at the Thompson boardinghouse to spend time with his roommate, John R. Pease, a cousin from Vermont. The Vermonter could not speak or write grammatically and as a conversationalist left much to be desired. Sometimes Rutherford would attend a country dance or try out his German on local immigrants. He even helped collect money for a local telegraph office "so we shall be within speaking distance of the great world." Mostly, however, he eased the tedium of village life with reading Shakespeare, writing in his diary, daydreaming, or worrying.

But Rutherford's career was going nowhere. He would later look back on the time he spent in Lower Sandusky with regret. "Oh, the waste of those five precious years!" he exclaimed.

Seeking a Wife

At 24, Rutherford wanted to get married. He cautiously courted the gracious Fanny Griswold Perkins, a blue-eyed, 21-year-old from Connecticut. But when he hinted at a desire to marry her, she was evasive. His overly gentlemanly approaches led to rebuffs, no real answer, and a feeling of failure.

Tormented by his confused feelings of love, Rutherford wrote in his diary on December 23, 1846, "I am almost wholly worthless. . . . I feel as if something was approaching in the future which is to determine my fortunes hereafter, and over which I have no control." He was on the verge of an apparent psychological crisis.

Suffering from throat trouble and chronic coughing, Rutherford was edgy, unable to concentrate, and lost interest in the world. He would wander around the village and weep inexplicably. He feared he might be going crazy and might follow his sister to the asylum. Finally, he unburdened his fears to a family friend, who sent him to doctors. They advised Rutherford to begin a more active life. He immediately took this advice to heart; he decided to volunteer for the then-raging war with Mexico.

Rutherford's support of the Mexican-American War contradicted all of the family's Whig principles — (the party had condemned the war as "most unnatural, ruinous and unnecessary"). Rutherford himself had spoken of the war as no more than an attempt by southern slaveowners to grab power and territory. Now he talked himself out of those views.

Rutherford understood his actions grew from the frustrations of his love life. "I must sow my wild oats," he said. "Had I married, as I wished I had, a year ago, I am persuaded this would not have occurred. My health would have been safe and myself a well-behaved civilian, instead of a rough volunteer." Soldiering, he figured, would distract him from his need to "sow wild oats."

To his family, Rutherford's decision sparked near panic, particularly from his sister. Uncle Sardis, however, kept calm. He understood the need to protect Rutherford's feelings. Sardis got Rutherford to agree to abide by the decision of two Cincinnati physicians on the best course for his health. These doctors, cued by Sardis, insisted that Rutherford needed fish oil, snakeroot, whiskey, and bleeding, but especially relaxation and a northern climate. To the great relief of his family, he took the advice and withdrew from the volunteers.

The incident led Rutherford to take control of his life. He decided to find out once and for all whether Fanny Perkins would marry him. He traveled to Connecticut and boldly broached the subject to her. They talked, deciding that his insistence on living in Ohio and her reluctance to leave Connecticut presented an insurmountable barrier. Relieved, they both laughed and joked. He wished her luck in choosing a husband. She said she would be glad to pay her respects to the future Mrs. Hayes. And then they parted as friends. ". . . So ends my first love affair," Rutherford wrote in his diary.

To Texas and Back

Late in 1848, at his uncle's suggestion, Rutherford and Sardis accepted an invitation to visit Kenyon classmate Guy Bryan's Texas plantation. After they had both campaigned in Ohio for Whig presidential candidate General Zachary Taylor and had seen him elected, they set off on the trip. The 3½-month stay in Texas, much of it spent traveling over the frontier on horseback, fortified Rutherford's sympathy for and appreciation of southerners.

When he and Sardis returned in March 1849 to Lower Sandusky, Rutherford decided to leave the village for bigger horizons. He would try his hand at law in what was then the biggest city in the West: Cincinnati, Ohio.

CINCINNATI LAWYER

On Christmas Eve 1849, 27-year-old Rutherford Hayes presented himself at the door of a boardinghouse on Pearl Street in Cincinnati. "A stranger seeking room among the brethren of the green [carpet] bag" is how he described himself. Rutherford understood that he might face hard times for the first few years. But he had earlier satisfied himself that "an attorney of my years and calibre would be likely to get business enough to pay office rent." After an introduction to an established lawyer did not produce the expected partnership, Rutherford set out on his own. He rented half an office for $10 a month on Third Street.

Rutherford and his office-mate, John C. Herron, who would one day become President William Howard Taft's father-in-law, used the office for living quarters. "We sleep on little hard mattresses in a little room cooped off from one end of our office. Quite like college life over again," Rutherford said. He waited three weeks before his first client came through the door. A coal merchant paid Rutherford five dollars to defend a suit in commercial court.

Business was slow at first, so Rutherford enjoyed himself and at the same time won clients and friends. He joined local societies and attended leading Episcopalian and Presbyterian churches on alternate weekends. He became a member of the Sons of Temperance, an association devoted to condemning the evils of drinking alcohol. In speeches to the group, he said he was mostly sincere about temperance, though he did drink his share of wine at another group he joined, the Literary Club of Cincinnati. At the meetings of this organization, Rutherford was exposed to the new ideas of his time. Later, he said that meeting the collection of young intellectuals, including some outstanding freethinkers and abolitionists, was the "most educational adventure" of his life.

Choosing Lucy

After moving to Cincinnati, Rutherford frequently dropped in to see Lucy Ware Webb, whom he had first met four years earlier in Delaware. Lucy was then 15 years old. Rutherford's mother had met Lucy's family and had decided the "bright-eyed" girl would make a good wife for her son. Lucy's mother agreed, but at that time Lucy was too young for him.

Rutherford had not given Lucy much thought when he first met her. Even after arriving in Cincinnati, he briefly dated a fashionable, sophisticated woman. But then he became more attracted to the more down-to-earth Lucy and started to visit her often after she graduated from Wesleyan Female College in Cincinnati.

One Friday evening in 1851, Rutherford arrived at Lucy's in high spirits. After spending the evening visiting with old acquaintances who lived nearby, they returned to Lucy's home and talked freely. Then, impulsively, Rutherford grasped her hand and said, "I love you." Because she did not seem to understand what he was saying, he repeated the words slowly: "I love you." Lucy was not startled. Instead, a puzzled expression of pleasure came to her face. She seemed most beautiful to Rutherford at that moment. She returned the pressure of his hand, and he knew then that Lucy was his. "I must confess, I like you very well," she said in soft tones. So it was decided that they would be married. All this Rutherford recorded dutifully in his diary.

The wedding took place on December 30, 1852, at the Webb home in Cincinnati. The couple would live happily together for over 36 years.

Hayes for the Defense

Rutherford's fortunes were beginning to brighten. On January 16, 1852, he had lost his first trial in criminal court, but he had won the respect of the judge. Although his client had been given a three-year prison sentence, Rutherford conducted

An 1852 wedding photograph of Rutherford and his wife, Lucy Ware Webb. She was a strong influence on Hayes, particularly in shaping his opposition to slavery in the years just after their marriage. (Library of Congress.)

himself so well that the judge appointed him to represent a poor servant girl charged with murder.

Rutherford recognized immediately the opportunity that this case afforded him. "It is *the* criminal case of the term. Will attract more notice than any other, and if I am well prepared, will give me a better opportunity to exert and exhibit whatever pith there is in me than any case I ever appeared in." It would also be the most important case of his legal career. The defendant was Nancy Farrer, a mentally unstable woman suspected of poisoning four people in two families who hired her as a maid.

Farrer, the daughter of an alcoholic father and a mother who considered herself the wife of Christ, pleaded not guilty. Despite Rutherford's spirited defense, the jury convicted her of murder and she was sentenced to hang. Rutherford appealed to the Ohio Supreme Court, putting forth a moving plea of insanity supported by medical evidence. In his speech to the court, he stated:

> The calamity of insanity is one which may touch very nearly the happiness of the best of our citizens. We all know that in some of its thousand forms it has carried grief and agony unspeakable to many a happy home. We must all wish to see such rules in regard to it established as would satisfy an intelligent man if, instead of this friendless girl, his own sister or his own daughter were on trial.

These words, recalling his own family's brush with insanity, led the court to decide that Farrer did not know right from wrong. Accordingly, she was sent to an asylum instead of the gallows. Thus saving her life, Rutherford earned acclaim and recognition as a capable lawyer.

The Farrer case became a landmark in the development of legal concepts of criminal responsibility. During the trial, Rutherford went to his sister's house to tell her about his actions in the Ohio Supreme Court. He mentioned to her the "golden opinions of his legal brethren" of his performance in court. Fanny was obviously proud. He was so relieved and happy he had met her high expectations for success that he broke down and cried.

Mental Illness

In Hayes' day, insanity was still widely viewed with fear and revulsion. Mental disturbances were traditionally believed to have supernatural origins. People acted strangely, it was thought, because they were "possessed" by demons and spirits. This misunderstanding led to the idea that cruelty was justified in treatment of the mentally sick, who were supposedly not fully human. In early asylums, they were routinely chained and locked out of sight. In colonial America, the mentally ill were driven from towns, sold for farm labor, or forced into poor houses.

It was a long time before the idea that the insane should be treated humanely took hold. Benjamin Rush, a physician and signer of the Declaration of Independence, advocated protection of the rights of the insane. Little changed, however, until Dorothea Dix, a teacher from Maine, discovered that in Massachusetts the insane were being jailed along with common criminals. She then launched a crusade in the 1840s that led to the establishment of many large state-supported institutions to house victims of mental illness. This led to improvements in care, but the so-called mental hospitals unexpectedly brought new problems. The sick lived in isolation, far from family and relatives, and some became victims of the old forms of maltreatment and neglect.

It was not until the 20th century that mental disorder was recognized as a treatable illness, much like influenza or cancer. This view came to be accepted internationally as scientific research began to show that social surroundings and childhood experiences influence mental well-being. This helped take away the mystery from mental illness, accelerating improvements in care and advancing understanding in a related area—legal ideas about criminal insanity.

Chapter 3

Prelude to Civil War

Whoever it was who abandoned the child on the steps of the Hayes home is not known. Perhaps the three-story townhouse at 383 Sixth Street in Cincinnati was chosen because the ornamental arches over the windows made it look fancier than the plainer homes on either side. Perhaps it was Hayes' reputation for sympathy to the blacks that brought the child to his doorstep.

In any case, it was suppertime on the evening of October 14, 1854, when Anna, the family's German maidservant, found a box at the front door. Investigating, she found it contained a naked, black infant. Startled, Anna cried out as she carried the box inside to Rutherford. With the help of antislavery activists, and after some trouble, he was finally able to place the baby in an orphanage.

The incident merits only 55 words in Rutherford's diary. But to historians, it has taken on symbolic importance. "The general unsolved problem of Negro slavery in America had been placed, so to speak, right on his doorstep," a biographer wrote. Placing the baby at the Hayes home could have reflected public recognition of a change in Rutherford's view toward slavery. His ideas about slavery had changed over the years, and he now felt strongly enough about the subject to support antislavery activists, the abolitionists. His new views led him to work against slavery and to develop attitudes that he would maintain decades later as a politician and President.

Rutherford changed his views about slavery for many reasons. Probably the one that had the most influence was Lucy's support of abolition. For her, slavery broke the laws of God. She acquired antislavery values from one of her grandfathers, who gave his slaves their freedom upon his death. Her father, upon inheriting slaves in Kentucky, voluntarily set them free.

Lucy's influence came to bear as Rutherford was exposed, for the first time, to realities of slavery he had not seen as a guest on a Texas plantation or heard from Harvard theorists. Slavery was outlawed in Ohio, but federal laws protected a slaveowner's "property" rights in all states. The laws threatened fines and jail for anyone who tried to help a runaway slave. So, when slaves fled north across the Ohio River to the border city of Cincinnati, southern slaveowners could pursue them mercilessly. In Cincinnati, it was common to see frightened black men and women, sometimes with children, pursued like animals, beaten, and dragged back to the South.

TAKING SIDES

Despite possible threats to his livelihood as a lawyer, Rutherford volunteered his services to help fugitive slaves. From 1853 onward, he would give legal assistance to blacks brought to him by the "Underground Railroad," an illegal organization that helped runaway slaves escape to Canada. Most cases generated little publicity, but a few became public dramas in the antislavery movement.

Such a case occurred in March 1855. It involved an escaped slave, Rosetta Armstrong. Armstrong's slave master, the Reverend Henry M. Dennison, had her arrested and brought to court in a bid to reclaim his property. But using a loophole in the federal Fugitive Slave Law, Rutherford and other lawyers fought the claim and won her freedom. A newspaper correspondent at the trial attributed the decision to Rutherford's "eloquent and masterly closing speech." The reporter for the Columbus *Columbian* said the audience's appreciation of his remarks "was manifest from their breathless silence during its delivery, their unrestrainable applause at its close, and the congratulations which the young orator received from a large number of his brethren at the bar."

Joys and Sorrows

Early in his marriage, Rutherford recorded in his diary, "A better wife I never hoped to have. This is indeed life. . . . Blessings on his head who first invented marriage." The couple had their first child, Birchard "Birchie" Austin, on November 4, 1853. He was followed three years later by a second son, Webb Cook. So occupied was Rutherford with his blossoming career, however, that he hardly had time for the family, barely seeing them except at meal times and Sundays.

With his growing prominence as a lawyer, Rutherford looked for a place to better profit from his career. He bought into a law firm under Richard Corwine. When lawyer William Rogers, a Kenyon classmate and friend, joined them in 1853, the firm was called "Corwine, Hayes & Rogers." Rutherford enjoyed the work, telling Sardis, "The business is large and very varied. I attend to the litigated business exclusively."

The death of Rutherford's sister, however, marred this period of happiness. On June 16, 1856, Fanny gave birth to twins, both of whom died. She suffered infection and complications from the births that left her in critical condition. Rutherford went to her bedside in Columbus and was able to talk to her when her mind was clear. He hoped she would recover, but she died on July 16.

"The dearest friend of my childhood—the affectionate adviser, the confidante of all my life—the one I loved best is gone," Rutherford wrote in his diary. He poured his sorrow out in letters to his Texas friend, Guy Bryan: "Oh what a blow it is! . . . All plans for the future, all visions of success, have embraced her as essential to complete them. . . . My heart bleeds and tears flow as I write."

His strong bonds to Lucy, the demands of his work, and a growing interest in politics seemed to help Rutherford overcome his grief. He was particularly caught up in the excitement over the presidential election of 1856. Vowing always to keep Fanny's memory as an inspiration to his growth, he recovered his balance.

BEFORE THE STORM

The years before the Civil War were marked by near chaos in politics. Compromises attempting to settle the slavery dispute during the 1850s failed one after another. Economic competition between the industrial North and the agricultural South increased the general bitterness. The political parties tried to cope with the growing frictions. The Whig Party, which Rutherford had supported, fell on hard times, losing membership because its compromises on slavery satisfied neither northern nor southern members. Although the other major party, the Democrats, did not fare much better, it managed to survive.

Numerous parties sprang up to fill the void left by the dying Whig Party. Among them were the Republicans, who wanted to weaken slavery by confining it to the South. Like many other northern Whigs, Rutherford settled on the new

Republican Party, which he helped establish in Ohio. When the Republicans put up John Frémont for President in 1856, Rutherford lent his enthusiastic support. Frémont lost to Democrat James Buchanan, who was soft on slavery. Buchanan's election, however, calmed anxieties over the issue—but only for a while.

Tempers soon rose higher than ever. Northerners who hated slavery learned they could do little about it through normal channels. The U.S. Supreme Court, in the Dred Scott decision of 1857, ruled that slaves were moveable property. The ruling opened the western portion of the country to slavery and slammed the door on any chance for a peaceful change. Two years later, extreme abolitionist John Brown and 18 followers, including five blacks, raided Harper's Ferry, Virginia. They tried to spark a widespread slave uprising but failed. Plantation owners saw the attack as proof that the antislavery movement in the North posed a deadly threat. They became more united and warlike than ever.

Solicitor Hayes

Rutherford waited and watched carefully for a chance to run for an elective office. He considered trying for a judgeship and running for Congress, but in each instance he decided to wait. The right moment arrived in December 1858, when the city solicitor of Cincinnati was killed in a train accident. The best lawyer's job in Cincinnati at the time, as Rutherford described it, was suddenly up for grabs. The city council met on December 9 to elect a replacement. On the eighth ballot, the council settled on Rutherford B. Hayes, giving him the post by a mere one-vote majority. This close call would be followed by many others in his career, giving Hayes a reputation for political luck in winning close elections.

Rutherford's mother greeted his victory with characteristic grimness. "If you wish to be happy, never aspire to political honors," Sophia said. "They are nothing but vanity and vexation of spirit." But Lucy and Sardis were elated. "So far, so good," Sardis wrote in a letter.

Serving as the city's legal expert suited Rutherford well. His care in rendering opinions to the mayor or city council won even more praise. The mayor referred to Rutherford as "our very competent Solicitor." Hayes also made a special gesture to demonstrate that he intended to serve with great honesty. On winning the job, Rutherford dissolved his ties to his law firm. He was satisfied that the $3,500 annual salary as city solicitor would provide a comfortable living. This sort of behavior set a high standard for ethics that Rutherford would maintain throughout his political career.

When he came up for re-election as city solicitor in April 1859, Rutherford won easily, and with the largest majority of any of the Republican candidates for municipal office. He felt good about the victory and gently teased his mother when he wrote, "I hope you are not cast down about my election here. . . . It will, I hope, not prove my ruin."

Enjoying Life

In February 1860 Rutherford told Sardis he was "not working very hard — not working much. I earn my salary, I am sure, and am therefore conscience clear. . . . I never enjoyed life better." Now family became Rutherford's main concern. Sunday scenes typified the Hayes' home life. Lucy would spend the day reading to her widowed mother, Maria Webb, who lived with them. The boys, now three of them with the birth in 1858 of Rutherford Platt, might shoot marbles. Rutherford played with his sons, telling them how it used to be when he was a little boy. He jested that he was now in the "boy business."

Rutherford did not participate in national politics at this time. He stayed home during the 1860 Republican National Convention in Chicago, when the party nominated Illinois lawyer Abraham Lincoln that year as its presidential candidate. Although he favored the choice, he showed no great enthusiasm for the contest. In February 1861, as Lincoln was on his way East to become President, Rutherford and Lucy were among the delegates to welcome him to Cincinnati. Rutherford remarked on Lincoln's awkward appearance. "When he bows," said Rutherford, ". . . his body breaks in two at the hips — there is a bend of the knees at a queer angle. It's good."

Fort Sumter

Lincoln's election triggered the rebellion of several southern states. They carried out their threat to break away, or secede, from the Union if the antislavery Republicans won the presidency. Rutherford recorded his concern on learning of the secession, the break-up of the Union, saying that "a war of conquest" by the North should be avoided. Two weeks later he wrote, "Six states have 'seceded.' *Let them go.*" He imagined that two Americas, one of free men and the other of slaves and owners, could coexist. There might be border fighting, but open warfare could be avoided. These views reflected wishful thinking, sentiments shared by a number of prominent Republicans on the eve of the Civil War. Lincoln, however, who had never been an abolitionist, refused to accept the secession. He hoped a policy of delay would allow tempers to cool.

Events soon overtook these hopes, sweeping Rutherford along with them. On April 1, 1861, he lost his re-election bid as city solicitor. The national crisis had triggered a backlash against the Republicans, as people blamed them for the frightening situation in the country. The entire Republican ticket in Cincinnati lost, though Rutherford was defeated by only a small margin.

Rutherford returned briefly to the private practice of law. But cannon blasts from South Carolina on April 12, 1861, changed everything. On that day the self-proclaimed Confederate States of America fired on the federal garrison at Fort Sumter, sparking war between North and South. President Lincoln immediately issued a call for 75,000 volunteers.

The day the news of Fort Sumter reached the Hayes family the little boys marched around the house beating their drums and shooting make-believe rifles. Sophia "read vigorously" the Old Testament. Maria Webb quietly grieved. At nearly 40, Rutherford could easily have left the fighting to younger men, but he was caught up in war fever. Within weeks he decided, with Lucy's blessing, to join the volunteers. He prepared by drilling with an informal unit made up of members of the Literary Club. His Kenyon classmate, Stanley Matthews, now Judge Matthews, decided to join with him. They agreed this "was a just and necessary war and that it demanded the whole power of the country," Rutherford wrote in his diary. "I would prefer to go into it if I knew I was to die, or be killed in the course of it, than to live through and after it without taking any part in it," he also wrote.

Chapter 4

"Pleasure Tour" Soldier

Colonel Rutherford B. Hayes, commander of the 23rd Ohio Volunteer Regiment, shouted to his men, and hundreds of Union soldiers responded by surging up the wooded slopes of South Mountain toward the enemy lines. When they emerged from the trees onto a cornfield, the Confederates opened fire from behind a stone fence. Rutherford, fearing his outnumbered forces could not stand long against the heavy volley, ordered a charge. The men dashed forward, pushing the enemy back.

Rutherford then ordered another charge; but just as he gave the command, a musketball slammed into his upper left arm. He sank to the ground, overcome by faintness. For a few moments he lay on the battlefield, 20 feet behind the lines. Seeing some men run back toward the woods, Rutherford believed his troops were retreating. He struggled to his feet and ordered them to hold their ground.

As the bullets whipped past, a sergeant approached and asked, "I am played out; please let me leave." Rutherford pointed with his sword to his bloodied arm. "Look at this. Don't talk about being played out," he yelled. "There is your place in line." Moments later, again overcome by faintness, he sank back to the ground.

This idealized drawing, by 23rd Ohio Volunteer Regiment soldier Joseph A. Joel, shows the wounded Hayes in the left foreground. Two soldiers with a horse have come to the aid of their commander. The artist depicted the ground as being flatter and more open than it really was. (Library of Congress.)

Rutherford then struck up a conversation with a wounded Confederate soldier who lay near him on the battlefield. "You came a long way to fight us," Rutherford said. The Confederate asked where Rutherford was from. "I am from Ohio," he answered. "Well," said the Confederate, "You came a good ways to fight us." Rutherford then gave the man a message for Lucy in case he died.

After this exchange, somehow characteristic of the gentlemanly Colonel Hayes, a lieutenant led him out of gunfire range and laid him down behind a log. Later, he was taken to a field hospital. In the meantime, his regiment fought on, winning honors on that September 14 of 1862.

Rutherford's troops broke the Confederate line. Elsewhere in the same battle, other Union forces triumphed as well. But it was Colonel Hayes' 23rd that had borne the brunt of the fighting that day in Maryland, suffering 130 casualties, including 32 killed. Glowing reports about the regiment appeared in the newspapers. The generals heaped praise on Rutherford. It was among his proudest moments in the war.

OHIO VOLUNTEER

Rutherford's Civil War career began on June 9, 1861, when he joined the 23rd Ohio Volunteer Regiment with the rank of major. His friend, Stanley Matthews, became a lieutenant colonel and his brother-in-law, Dr. Joseph Webb, a surgeon in the same unit. All three joined the regiment—900 to 1,000 men strong—as it was being assembled near Columbus.

Rutherford immediately found that he enjoyed army life. The soldiers' drill parades filled him with excitement and pride. He was much happier than he could be, he wrote to Lucy, "fretting away in the old office near the Court House. It is living."

The soldiers trained until late July, rising before breakfast to drill for an hour, then drilling again in late morning and in the afternoon. Regular army men took charge of the training, shaping the volunteers into soldiers, which was no simple task. Rutherford knew little about warfare, but he learned quickly. When he found himself in situations where he had not learned what to do, he quickly improvised.

When orders came for the regiment to move out, Rutherford went to the train station with Lucy and her mother. "I saw them watching me as I stood on the platform on the rear of the last car as long as they could see me," he said. "Their eyes swam. I kept my emotion under control enough not to melt into tears." The regiment traveled for three days by train, foot, and riverboat to the Kanawha Valley, in the area that would eventually be the state of West Virginia.

"A Pleasure Tour"

For much of the war, the 23rd was engaged in holding action, crisscrossing the Appalachian Mountains in patrols and campaigns. Most of the time the regiment fought little battles, chased snipers and guerrillas (called bushwackers), and patrolled mountain roads. This kind of warfare was hard to endure, dirty, and dull. Rutherford, however, enjoyed the whole affair. "These marches and campaigns in the hills of western Virginia will always be among the pleasantest things I can remember. The feeling that I am where I ought to be is a full compensation for all that is sinister, leaving me free to enjoy it as if on a pleasure tour." Horse riding and outdoor "physical enjoyments of this sort are worth a war," he said. He also grew a full beard.

Only months after reaching the front-line areas did Rutherford get a taste of a real battle. At Carnifix Ferry in western Virginia, he led several companies of the regiment against a Confederate force dug in along the Gauley River. They never came very close to the enemy. Mostly, the Confederates fired 50 feet over the attackers' heads in the uneven terrain. Although casualties were light, the action gave Rutherford a chance to find out how he would react under fire. Would he want to run away? He reported in a letter to Lucy that he was no more nervous than what "I have often felt before beginning an important lawsuit."

Battles brought out an aggressive, daring side of Rutherford that seemed to give him greater self-confidence. His nerve was sustained by a conviction that he was fighting what he called a "holy war" against slavery.

In the fall of 1861, Rutherford was appointed army advocate general. Because the job dealt with discipline cases behind the lines, he was disappointed with it. Although the position provided comforts and extra pay, he missed the fighting. He requested reassignment to a front-line position, where he stayed until the end of the war.

Lessons of War

Rutherford studied war manuals and questioned army regulars on the art of warfare. But after he observed military professionals make foolish decisions, he began to rely more on his own analyses of situations. "Good sense and energy are the qualities required," he decided. Rutherford seemed to have both, plus ambition. He made sure his superiors knew when he did well and avoided bringing attention to himself when he did not. During an attack early in the war at Giles Courthouse in Virginia, Rutherford advanced too far into enemy lines and was forced to retreat, escaping "by a miracle." He was guilty of rashness and knew it, but he angrily defended his actions to his superiors. To his credit, he learned from his mistakes and became among the most professional of soldiers.

Rutherford, pictured in his uniform, served four years as a Union soldier. He rose from the rank of major to brevet (honorary) major general of the volunteer forces and was the first President since James Monroe to be wounded in battle. (Library of Congress.)

Rutherford's most valuable asset was his understanding of the way men think. He commanded with a firm hand, but gave orders thoughtfully. The men trusted him, knowing he would not order them to make unnecessary marches or endure severe hardship. His feats in battle and his competence led to promotions to regimental, brigade, and division commander. And, just after the war, he was promoted to brevet (honorary) major general of the volunteers.

A Leader of Men

Rutherford's ability as a leader became famous. A bright, 18-year-old staff sergeant named William McKinley (who would make history himself by becoming the 25th President of the United States) said Rutherford was "the sunny, agreeable, the kind, the generous, the gentle gentleman" off the battlefield. But his "whole nature seemed to change in battle," becoming "intense and ferocious." Another soldier recalled that during a battle in May of 1862, he saw Rutherford come riding at a gallop down the battle lines, waving his sword, "the grand anger of battle flashing in his eyes. It puts fight in us to see Colonel Hayes riding at full gallop towards the rebel battery. . . . Who could not follow him in battle."

It was such a moment of gallantry during the assault on South Mountain that the bullet hit Rutherford. He was treated for his wounds by his brother-in-law, who saved the arm from amputation. From his bed, he sent a telegram to Lucy to let her know he survived. "I am here, come to me, I shall not lose my arm," it read.

On receiving the news, Lucy entrusted the children to relatives and left the next morning to join her husband. After searching for him for days, she located him in a hospital and stayed several weeks, helping care for him and for other wounded soldiers. When Rutherford recovered enough to travel, they returned to Ohio. After seven weeks there, he returned to the war, which, he said, was "like getting home again after a long absence."

Lucy visited Rutherford a number of times in lulls between fighting. Sometimes she brought the children, including a fourth son, Joseph, born in late 1861. On one of these visits, Lucy and the boys lived in a log cabin at the regiment's wintering camp. Mother and sons "rowed skiffs, fished, built dams, sailed little ships and enjoyed camp life generally," Rutherford recorded. On a second visit to the camp, little Joseph became ill with dysentery and died. A fifth wartime son, George, was born in 1864. He died of scarlet fever before the age of two.

War Brutality

From the early days of guerrilla-hunting patrols, Rutherford saw what the war was all about. The supporters of the Confederates, he decided, were the wealthy and the ignorant. The common southern soldier was tired of fighting a "rich man's war." He found the runaway slaves who entered the military camp daily to be more intelligent than most local white natives and thought they deserved a better life.

By 1862, only a year into the conflict, Rutherford grew increasingly harsh toward the hard-core rebels. "I am gradually coming to the opinion that this Rebellion can only be crushed by either the execution of all the traitors or the abolition of slavery." The rebellion would, in fact, not end before Lincoln's 1863 Emancipation Proclamation freeing the slaves and the Union victory two years after that.

Though Rutherford always believed he was fighting a righteous war, the hatred it created upset him. He once saw a Union general turn a family out in the cold and burn their home 10 minutes later. "There are enough 'brutal Rebels' no

History of Slavery

Slavery dates back to ancient times and was practiced in many parts of the world. Debtors, criminals, and captured enemies were among the many people who might be forced into slavery. Trade in captured West African natives came to the British colonies in America when, in 1619, a Dutch ship unloaded a cargo of blacks in Jamestown, Virginia, and they were enslaved. At first slavery was slow to take root in America. But with the cultivation of tobacco, and later of rice, sugar, and cotton on plantations in the South, the demand for labor rose sharply and the slave trade boomed. The total number of slaves in America jumped from 59,000 in 1714 to 263,000 in 1754, then to well over four million by the eve of the Civil War.

Opposition to slavery came late in history. Little was heard against the practice until the 18th century, when new ideas in Europe about the rights of man began to spark protests. Such leading figures of the American Revolution as Thomas Jefferson and Benjamin Franklin condemned slavery. Strict religious groups also opposed it for its unchristian qualities.

In America, the Quakers took the lead in fighting slavery. By 1804, they and other antislavery groups had persuaded all states north of Maryland to abolish the practice. Quakers also participated in the Underground Railroad, an illegal organization to free slaves and help them escape the country.

> In the South, some slaveowners responded to the antislavery movement by voluntarily freeing their slaves. But protests had little effect on the great plantations of the Deep South, which depended on slave labor. Though the Civil War brought an end to slavery in the United States, it would be practiced well into the 20th century, especially in parts of Africa, the Middle East, and Asia. In the Western Hemisphere, slavery was practiced in Cuba and Brazil until the 1880s.

doubt," he told Lucy, "but we have brutal officers and men too . . . and there are plenty of humane Rebels." When a general ordered the destruction of much of Lexington, Virginia, out of "crusading zeal," Rutherford was horrified. Using the pretext that the civilians had fired on his soldiers, the general permitted them to loot and burn the town, including its schools and church. Rutherford understood that the rampage turned the people against the Union cause.

Rutherford also began to see war as a political instrument—as Lincoln saw it. He understood that brutality would create divisions that people would have to overcome after the war, that the defeated must be lived with after victory.

CONGRESSMAN HAYES

When the Civil War was over, the honors Rutherford won and the wounds he suffered would serve political ends. Nationally, he would stand out for his war record. Bullets hit Rutherford three times, and he suffered other injuries when horses were shot out from under him. No President since

James Monroe, a Revolutionary War hero, had been wounded on the battlefield. Rutherford's popularity among the Ohio regiment would be a political asset in state elections. This was recognized when, in the fall of 1864, the local Republican Party nominated him for congressman from the Second (Cincinnati) District.

Hayes' nomination was largely the work of William Henry Smith, a newspaperman who had known and liked Rutherford before the war. Smith would also be crucial in later boosting Rutherford to the presidency. Nominating Rutherford at that moment served the party's immediate needs. Civilians had become pessimistic after expecting the war would be over six months after it started. Moreover, the war was not going well for the North in 1864. The Democrats had gained strength after Lincoln, a Republican, was elected President in 1860. Smith hoped Rutherford's fame as a soldier would swing the local race to the Republicans.

Rutherford wanted the seat in Congress, but he felt his duties as a soldier came first. He even stopped an attempt by the men of the regiment to organize a "Hayes for Congress" movement. He accepted the nomination—but on the condition that he would not leave the war to campaign. When Smith suggested he take a furlough to stump (go out and make speeches) for votes, Hayes wrote back:

> Friend Smith, your suggestion about getting a furlough to take the stump was certainly made without reflection. An officer fit for duty who at this crisis would abandon his post to electioneer for a seat in Congress ought to be scalped. You may feel perfectly sure I will do no such thing.

Without making any appearances in his district in Cincinnati, Rutherford won the election. Lincoln was pleased, seeing Hayes' victory as a sign of public support for his own re-election the following November.

Lincoln's Vision

When the Civil War ended in the spring of 1865, the South lay in ruins. Twisted railroad tracks, buildings reduced to heaps of rubble, and fields of burned crops marked the trail of the Union forces' final assault through the region. Altogether, more than 600,000 people died in the conflict, with another 400,000 wounded. The North suffered most of the casualties, including many among the 186,000 black soldiers who fought for the North. But the greatest hunger, disease, and displacement of the civilian population hit the South, where most of the fighting took place.

With slavery gone forever and the threat to the Union averted, President Lincoln surveyed the destruction. He believed it was time for the healing of wounds, bringing North and South together again. "With malice toward none; with charity for all . . . let us strive . . . to bind up the nation's wounds," Lincoln counseled. He never got a chance. On April 15, 1865, an unemployed actor killed Lincoln with a single shot to the back of his head.

The assassination shocked and horrified the nation, reminding it that the fighting may have stopped, but the deeper problems lived on. Rutherford, too, glimpsed the future. "The work of Reconstruction requiring so much statesmanship [is] just begun," he wrote on the day after Lincoln's death. He spoke of Lincoln's greatness and wondered how the tragedy of war would affect the future.

Chapter 5

Ohio Politician

After Lincoln's assassination presidential leadership fell to Vice-President Andrew Johnson, a man of lesser ability than Lincoln. Johnson, a Tennesseean and a Democrat who had been chosen by Lincoln for the vice-presidency because he refused to support secession, tried to carry out Lincoln's plan of reuniting the North and South. During the period following the Civil War, which came to be known as "Reconstruction," Johnson opted for mild treatment of the defeated southerners. He pardoned Confederate soldiers, refused to execute military and civilian leaders, and let whites re-establish control of the southern states. But the plan produced unexpected results. Whites quickly passed "black laws" forcing former slaves to accept severe new restrictions. The laws horrified northerners, who saw them as cancelling the effects of the war the North had given so much to win.

Johnson's soft approach triggered determined opposition in Congress. The strongest faction, known as the Radical Republicans, had little sympathy for the South. "Humble the proud traitors," said Radical Republican Representative Thaddeus Stevens. The Radicals wanted to punish Confederate leaders as well as protect former slaves and loyal whites. This stand reflected sincere moral concern for the blacks. It also grew from another motivation—the Radicals expected blacks to vote Republican. Political power was at stake.

RADICAL CONGRESSMAN

Rutherford resigned from the military on June 8, 1865, four years to the day from his becoming a soldier. He packed up his sword, chest, and flags, gave orders for the transportation back home of his favorite horse, Old Whitey, and bid farewell to his men. He would tell a veterans' gathering years later that army life was "the best years of our lives." Traveling through Ohio, he then headed for Washington to take his seat in Congress.

Congressman Hayes voted consistently with the Radicals, who came to dominate the Republican Party. When angered by Johnson's resistance to their proposals for punishing the South, the Radicals demanded that he be impeached (put on trial for alleged crimes). Rutherford voted for approval of the move. Generally, however, the Ohio congressman stayed in the background, rarely speaking in debates. Privately, he entertained reservations about the more extreme aspects of the Radical program.

In the fall of 1866, Rutherford campaigned for re-election to Congress on the Radical platform—which almost cost him the election. His personal popularity brought victory, but the state elected mostly Democrats that year, including a Democratic governor. Ohioans also turned down a proposed state constitutional amendment to permit blacks to vote in Ohio. Clearly, Hayes' views on Reconstruction were not an asset that year.

Displeasure with Congress

Congress turned out to be a disappointment for Rutherford. He felt his most significant accomplishment was as chairman of the unimportant Library Committee. In this position, he persuaded Congress to approve the merger of the Smithsonian Institution library and the Library of Congress. He also won authorization for the Library of Congress, originally only a branch of Congress, to serve other branches of government and the public. These changes helped make the Library of Congress the great institution it is today.

For these small rewards, Rutherford had to be apart from Lucy and his children, who stayed in Ohio. He also disliked being kept busy with trifling matters brought to him by the people of his home district. And private-interest groups treated him like their personal Washington lobbyist. The Ohio Wool Growers' Association, for example, expected him to unquestioningly support higher duties (taxes) on wool imports. When he balked, exercising his independence as a statesman, he was criticized. Dislike of these frictions led Rutherford to describe himself to Lucy as an "errand boy to one hundred fifty thousand people."

Hayes admired some of his colleagues in Congress, but disapproved of much of what he found. He particularly disliked the use of political office for personal gain. These years began what author Mark Twain called the "Gilded Age," a get-rich-quick period when financial and industrial tycoons wielded huge power over government and the booming American economy.

Many legislators profited from the nation's expansion through various schemes to swindle the public. Although Rutherford did not become involved in any of these schemes, he did not like the smell of corruption that tainted Congress. In a moment of frustration, he questioned whether he should continue in politics. "Politics is a bad trade. . . . Guess we'll quit," he wrote to Lucy.

This sentiment echoed those of Rutherford's mother, Sophia, who had died in October 1866 at the age of 74. She had wondered whether Rutherford would "be preserved from the vile and frivolous company" around him in Washington.

GOVERNOR HAYES

In late 1867 Rutherford received a letter that lifted his spirits. It came from William Henry Smith, the newspaperman who had been influential in his election to Congress. Now the secretary of state in Ohio, Smith wanted to know if Rutherford might be interested in becoming a candidate for governor. The Radicals who dominated the state Republican Party needed a candidate in favor of laws giving blacks suffrage (the right to vote). The person had to be of strong moral character, with a distinguished war record and not too closely indentified with the unpopular Radicals. Rutherford fit the bill.

After some hemming and hawing, Hayes accepted, resigned from Congress, and campaigned hard, giving 81 major speeches. The votes of war veterans in a few counties won the election for him on October 8, 1867. His success was marred only by the voters' rejection of a black suffrage amendment on the same ballot. Rutherford again had won on personal appeal, though his support of black voting rights went against popular sentiments.

After Hayes and his family moved into a new home in Columbus, he began his two-year term. The job suited him fine, even though the governor had relatively few powers, lacking even the right to veto, or reject, legislative acts. But Rutherford seemed to like best the respect he and "the governor's lady" received. "I am enjoying the new office," he wrote to Uncle Sardis. "It strikes me at a guess as the pleasantest I have ever had. Not too much work, plenty of time to read, good society, etc., etc."

Governor Hayes promoted a program of better state government, prevention of fraud in elections, and reform of jails, orphanages, and insane asylums. He also appointed Democrats to some state offices, in part out of political necessity, thereby achieving representation of the minority party on state boards and commissions. This practice paved the way for similar reforms of the federal government that Hayes would undertake as President.

A Second Term

Rutherford liked the governor's job well enough to run again in 1869. This time he won by a larger margin than before. During his second term, he sponsored the establishment of what would be Ohio State University and championed a money policy that would favor financial stability.

Rutherford's crowning achievement of his governorship was securing the Ohio legislature's acceptance of the 15th Amendment to the Constitution of the United States. The 15th Amendment states that a person's right to vote shall not be denied on the basis of "race, color, or previous conditions of servitude." Acceptance of this amendment in Ohio was considered vital to protecting the achievements of the Civil War.

The Republican Party also considered acceptance of the 15th Amendment fundamental to the party's continued dominance of national politics. If the amendment passed, and blacks had the right to vote in the South, they would generally choose the party of the Civil War, the Republicans. By securing the state of Ohio's approval of the 15th Amendment, Rutherford won the gratitude of his party—and Republican leaders would not soon forget.

The passage of the 15th Amendment gave Rutherford great satisfaction. It was to him a completion of his greatest political aim. He wrote to one of Lucy's brothers, saying, "The cause I enlisted for is completely mastered, and the new questions do not interest me." The "new questions" to which he referred included the industrial changes in the country, women's suffrage, and all other social, political, and economic ills. Nearing the end of his second term as governor, Rutherford was unwilling or unable to grapple with these problems. Instead, he awaited his return to private life "as hopefully as a school boy to his coming vacation."

A Difficult Refusal

One evening, just before the end of his governorship, Rutherford had already gone to bed when suddenly the front doorbell rang. He got up. A Republican state senator and a representative waited to see him.

"Well, I come to business at once," the senator said. "We want to make you senator."

With only a few weeks left in his term of office, Rutherford knew what he meant. Members of the Ohio Republican Party wanted to nominate him to run for the U.S. Senate. Rutherford had already indicated he would not run. Moreover, the Republican Party's nominating meeting, or caucus, had already committed itself to another candidate, present Senator John Sherman. The visitors, however, hoped they could change Rutherford's mind and oust Sherman, whom some party members disliked. The state senator hoped to persuade Rutherford to change his mind, telling him, "The man now elected Senator over the caucus will be the next President of the United States."

This was possible, Rutherford knew, but he told the visitors that it would dishonor the party to reverse its nomination. He urged them to stick with Sherman because to break the promise might split the Republican Party at a time when it needed unity to re-elect President Ulysses S. Grant, who had taken office after Andrew Johnson. He told the visitors he would not run "under any circumstances." They left, wondering why Rutherford would "throw away the senatorship."

Rutherford went back to bed. But that same night another visitor came, a prominent banker whose power represented strong assurance that Rutherford would be elected if he chose to run. Rutherford would not change his mind. "I can't honorably do it," he said.

Sherman was re-elected. He remembered Rutherford's refusal to run as a personal debt that he would repay one day soon.

Party Sacrifices

Hayes was back in politics within six months after leaving office. He stepped in to help shape a platform for the Republican National Convention that would renominate Grant for President. His service to the party was an act of loyalty at a time when the party was threatened with a split. It was also a snub to a faction of Liberal Republicans who wanted to back off the Radical program of Reconstruction in the South. Although Rutherford had friends in the Liberal movement, he preferred to remain in the regular party, believing—rightly as it turned out—that the Liberals had little chance of success at that time.

A few months later, Republican politicians convinced Rutherford to run for Congress in the Second District again. If he did not do so, they feared the party might lose Ohio to Horace Greeley, the presidential candidate endorsed by both the Democrats and the Liberal Republicans. But a strong Greeley vote in Cincinnati swept Rutherford to defeat, though Grant won nationally.

To the Republican Party, Rutherford's bid for office nevertheless represented a personal "sacrifice," and it owed him a debt of gratitude. Even so, the loss annoyed Rutherford. He was doubly annoyed when Grant later clumsily tried to reward him with an appointment to a minor federal post. This incident marked a low point in Rutherford's career. He declared he was finished with politics "definitely, absolutely and positively."

Rutherford now took up Uncle Sardis' offer to live in the tree-shaded mansion he had built at Spiegel Grove, on the outskirts of Fremont. At age 50, Rutherford was returning to the place formerly known as Lower Sandusky, where nearly three decades before he had hung out his shingle to begin his career in law.

The family settled in Fremont as the three older boys went off to college, leaving Rutherford and Lucy with the youngest children, Fanny, Scott, and Manning Force, all born after the war. Manning Force died in 1874. In that same year, Sardis passed away while Rutherford held his hand. Not long before his death he had told his nephew, "You have been a good boy," words which Rutherford liked to recall. Sardis left the home at Spiegel Grove to Rutherford along with much of his personal fortune, eventually worth about $500,000.

Rethinking Reconstruction

Rutherford made a remark in his diary on March 28, 1875, that marked a turning point in his thinking: "I doubt the ultra [Radical] measures being applied to the South." He was leaving the Radical line, recognizing that Reconstruction had not met with expectations. "Carpetbagger" governments, named after the carpetbag-carrying northerners who rushed south to take jobs in Reconstruction governments after the war, had forced the South to give power to blacks. Though a relatively small number of blacks held elective office as con-

After his second term as governor of Ohio, Rutherford vowed to leave politics. He settled on the family estate at Spiegel Grove in Fremont, Ohio. The home is now part of the Hayes Presidential Library and Museum. (Library of Congress.)

gressmen, senators, and state officials, the number was larger than at any time until civil rights campaigns of the 1950s reopened political opportunity to blacks. Battered by postwar economic troubles, white opposition, and their own corruption, however, many Reconstruction governments collapsed by themselves. One by one, they lost power to white-domination and control of the Democrats, the party of former slaveowners.

In states like Mississippi, the Ku Klux Klan and similar

white terrorist organizations pushed blacks out of power by burning their schools and churches, by murder, and by threats. In other states, such as Louisiana, blacks, unhappy with the poor performance of their state legislators, apparently helped vote out the Republican government. The policy of Reconstruction was obviously failing to sustain the achievements of the Civil War.

The political goals of the Civil War era were giving way to concerns about economic ills born in part from the inept and corrupt administration of President Grant. His poor leadership gave big business powers a free hand, which may have helped lead to a financial crisis and full-fledged depression in 1873. Under Grant, the Navy sold business to contractors, the Interior Department worked hand in hand with land speculators, and a group of revenue officers and liquor distillers cheated the government out of millions of dollars. The President himself was not tainted with graft, but public morality was at a new low. In despair, the people turned to the Democrats, who had never favored the Civil War. Republican influence began to wane.

Fortunately for Rutherford, he had been in retirement when the charges against Grant grew most serious. In the people's minds, he was not closely associated with the corruption of the Grant administration.

BACK IN POLITICS

Hayes, unable to keep out of the "political rut," was back in public life by early 1875. Ohio Republicans unanimously nominated him for a third term as governor. The office interested Rutherford, but he went through his usual qualms about politics, at first declining the offer. Eventually, however, he talked himself into it. "A third term would be a distinction—a feather I would like to wear. No man ever had it in Ohio. Letters tell me I am really wanted," he wrote in his diary that March. He then went on to give a number of reasons why he could not possibly run for office. He recorded, "I have said decidedly no to all who have approached me."

But more than the Ohio governorship was at stake. Some party leaders believed that if Rutherford could win a third term as governor, he would have a chance of winning the Republican nomination for President. "How wild!" Rutherford wrote of these suggestions. "What a queer lot we are becoming! Nobody is out of reach of that mania." But he soon caught the presidential bug. On June 2, 1875, he accepted the nomination for the governorship.

With Rutherford being seen as a possible presidential candidate, his campaign for governor took on new importance. The issues he pushed in Ohio would now follow him more than ever before. With these factors in mind, he chose to campaign on issues of national appeal. Rutherford called for "honest money for all, and free schools for all." The "free schools" promise grew out of an Ohio law allowing inmates to have Catholic chaplains at prisons and hospitals. Republicans and Protestants opposed the law, fearing the next step might be a law forcing the state to pay for running Catholic schools. "Honest money" was an issue put forth in opposition to the Democrats, who wanted the government to respond to economic problems by printing more "greenback" dollar notes. Rutherford opposed the plan, favoring "hard money," a monetary system based on gold and silver. If he won with this issue, the Republicans would then know that they should become the "hard money" party.

Hayes ran energetically, winning a third term by a few

thousand votes. This victory helped Rutherford grow in political stature in the eyes of Republican leaders.

The Hayes family was excited about the prospect of the presidency. At home, Winnie Monroe, the family's maidservant and the daughter of a slave, overcame her usual moodiness and made an elaborate Thanksgiving dinner. It was her way of showing her enthusiasm for rising with them to "the top of the ladder."

On the eve of his election as governor, Hayes had already begun to look ahead, but with more concern than Winnie. He knew better what hurdles and trials he might face. He wrote:

> If victorious, I am likely to be pushed for the Republican nomination for President. This would make my life a disturbed and troubled one until the nomination, six or eight months hence. If nominated the stir would last until November a year hence. Defeat in the next Presidential election is almost a certainty.

Chapter 6

Wheeling and Dealing

The vast crowd of excited delegates to the Republican National Convention of 1876 assembled in a huge hall in Cincinnati. Seated in the four-acre expanse, thousands of people listened to the formal nominating speeches. One after another of the state delegates mounted the platform to praise their favorite presidential candidate. The next to last speaker was former Ohio Governor Edward F. Noyes. Standing before the convention, he put forward the name of Rutherford B. Hayes, "a man who, during the dark and stormy days of the rebellion, when those who are invincible in peace and invisible in battle were uttering brave words to cheer their neighbors on, himself in the forefront of battle, followed his leaders and his flag until the authority of our government was reestablished." This praise was an indirect jab at James G. Blaine, another contender for the nomination and a U.S. senator from Maine who had stayed home during the war. Applause for Hayes' nomination was generous.

After one more nominating speech, the convention adjourned until 10:00 A.M. the next day. The stage was now set for the final act of a political drama that would launch a candidate into the race for President of the United States.

BEHIND THE SCENES

In March of 1876, after the 750 delegates to the Ohio State Republican Convention endorsed Hayes as their candidate for President, influential figures began to maneuver behind the scenes on his behalf. The most effective of these men was the little-known William H. Smith, then general agent for a news agency. Using his contacts in the news media, Smith guided the Hayes movement, accurately predicting the winning ticket five months in advance of the national convention.

Hayes was confident that the "good purposes and the judgment, experience, and firmness" he possessed would serve him well in the presidency. He worked steadily but quietly with his supporters, keeping himself in the background. He tried not to seem too eager to be picked. "I must be passive," he said. He knew that being prominent would attract opponents to unite against him and lead to his defeat. Hayes wisely left the front-runner title to Blaine, whose links to scandal would lead to his downfall.

The Republicans knew they could only attract votes if they presented a candidate who stood solidly against corruption. One contender, New York Senator Roscoe Conkling was closely identified with the discredited Grant administration. So was Indiana Senator Oliver Morton, who otherwise boasted a solid record. Benjamin H. Bristow, former secretary of the treasury, had cracked down on federal corruption under Grant. But Bristow was not a regular party man and many delegates resented him. By elimination, that left Hayes, who was both untainted and free of ties with the Grant administration.

Sharp politicians realized before the convention that Hayes might win the nomination by default. But they hesitated to support him because of his lack of national standing.

Governor S. J. Kirkwood, in a letter written a month before the convention, acknowledged, "Hayes of Ohio would do, but nobody out of Ohio knows anything about him and we want a man with more than a state reputation."

During the convention, Hayes stayed in Columbus. As was the tradition at that time, presidential hopefuls did not attend their party's national convention. Instead they watched and waited. In Cincinnati, delegations supporting each candidate began working for votes. The Hayes delegation wisely kept a low profile, trying to keep on good terms with all groups. This tactic of arousing no opposition eventually helped make Hayes the second choice of almost everyone at the convention. On Monday, June 12, Rutherford's son Webb, who was attending the convention as an observer, telegraphed to his father: "GREATEST GOOD FEELING PREVAILS TOWARD YOU ON ALL SIDES . . . ALL FRIENDS—NO ENEMIES."

Many of the delegates from each state had already chosen a candidate, but no candidate had enough votes to win. As delegates sized up the situation, the Hayes momentum seemed to catch on. Late Thursday, the day after the nominations were made in the convention hall, Webb sent another message to his father: "GOVERNOR NOYES INSTRUCTS ME TO SAY THAT THE COMBINATIONS ARE VERY FAVORABLE."

The next morning, realizing he might win, Rutherford had written in his diary that if Blaine's support weakened:

> My chance, as a compromise candidate, seems to be better than any other. So now we are in suspense. I have kept cool and unconcerned to a degree that surprises me. . . . I feel that a defeat will be a great relief—a setting free from bondage. The great responsibility overpowers me.

Seventh-Ballot Win

On the first roll call vote on Friday, Blaine got 285 votes; Morton, 124; Bristow, 113; Conkling, 99; and Hayes, 61. Three other candidates received fewer votes. Needing 378 votes to win, Hayes ran a poor fifth on the first ballot. But no candidate gained significantly until the fifth ballot. At that point, the chairman of Michigan's 22-member delegation, which had been divided between Bristow, Blaine, and Hayes supporters, stood up to say, "Michigan . . . casts her 22 votes for Rutherford B. Hayes of Ohio."

The switch started a movement to Hayes, and he began to pick up other votes. But on the sixth ballot, Blaine supporters rallied, moving him to within 70 votes of victory. Hayes gained too, however, moving into second place with 113 votes, just ahead of Bristow's 111.

When the Blaine backers spread the word that they would make a final push on the seventh ballot, opposition delegates knew they had to act immediately. The roll was called. Blaine gained at first, but then Indiana withdrew Morton's name and gave 25 votes to Hayes. The anti-Blaine forces jumped to their feet, swinging hats and handkerchiefs and clapping loudly. Kentucky was next. The chairman withdrew Bristow's name and gave the state's votes to Hayes. Tumultuous applause broke out again. One after the other, states shifted to Hayes, and before anyone realized it, he had a majority. The final tally gave Blaine 351 votes; Bristow, 21; and Hayes, 384. The cheering lasted 10 to 15 minutes, then the nomination of Hayes was made unanimous.

The convention finished its work by nominating Congressman William A. Wheeler for Vice-President. In those days the candidate did not choose his own running mate. When months earlier Rutherford had first heard the New Yorker's name, he had asked, "Who is Wheeler?"

*Hayes and his vice-presidential running mate, Congressman
William A. Wheeler of New York, are shown in a campaign
banner. Wheeler, who was nominated by the party and was not
Rutherford's choice, would play a minor role in the Hayes
presidency.* (Library of Congress.)

Democrats for Tilden

Later in June, the Democrats met in St. Louis to choose their presidential candidate. For them the choice was simple: Samuel J. Tilden. The clean-shaven, silver-haired governor of New York was known for breaking New York City's notorious Boss Tweed bribery ring. Like Hayes, Tilden was a wealthy lawyer. But he lived as a bachelor and was known privately for his scholarly mind, legal intellect, and cold personality. His vice-presidential running mate was Senator Thomas A. Hendricks of Indiana.

CAMPAIGN PUSH

Both presidential candidates stayed in their home states during the campaign. They appeared infrequently in public because that was the way things were done then. The modern method of campaigning had not yet been adopted. Tilden, however, employed a new campaign technique. He opened a "newspaper popularity bureau" (a public relations agency), which had never been done before. With it, he broadcast his ideas and "image" with press releases. Taking an active role in making his campaign very effective, Tilden soon emerged as the more popular of the two candidates.

Hayes' campaign manager was the rather shady Zachary Chandler, a big-bellied man with bushy whiskers and flashy clothes who had served in Grant's Cabinet. His appointment was imposed on Rutherford by party regulars who felt pushed out because he had won the nomination. Chandler ran the campaign practically independent of Hayes. Much of the Republican campaign fund, to the annoyance of the Liberal Republicans and despite their objections, Chandler collected forcibly from federal employees.

Hayes stepped into the public light only once during the campaign. This was to attend the Centennial Exposition in Philadelphia, which on July 4, 1876, celebrated the 100th anniversary of American independence. Displayed at the exposition were all the latest wonders of science, including the newly invented telephone. When Rutherford arrived, he apparently made a rather bad impression on a *New York Times* reporter: "He wore a dreadfully shabby coat and a strikingly bad hat, all brushed the wrong way." The public seemed not to mind. Admirers mobbed Rutherford to shake his hand.

Letter of Acceptance

In a formal "Letter of Acceptance" to the Republican Party for getting the nomination, Rutherford made a bold promise to reform the spoils system of hiring employees for the national government. The arrangement, as it had worked for decades, allowed congressmen and the President to reward supporters with federal jobs rather than giving the positions to qualified applicants.

In his letter, Hayes also said it was his "inflexible purpose" not to be a candidate for a second term. This was a way to separate himself from the Grant-era corruption. The pledge insulted Grant, who had served a disastrous second term and in 1880 would try to be nominated for a third term. But it demonstrated Hayes' moral commitment not to build a personal empire. Hayes' campaign position on reform and corruption was close to that of Tilden's.

Although Hayes may have scored points on the corruption issue, it was still the issue of greatest strength for the Democrats. They could simply harp on the acknowledged corruption of the Grant administration. Furthermore, Tilden already wore the mantle of reform for his victories against Boss Tweed's huge criminal ring in New York City. The economy was also an issue for the Democrats. All they had to do was remind people of the nation's economic troubles under Grant's presidency.

In response to the big issues that Democrats had to wield against the Republicans, Hayes' campaign took a harsh tactic, assailing Tilden's character. The party spokesmen said he was sympathetic to the Confederates. This was simple character assassination, "waving the bloody shirt," a Republican tactic of questioning the Democrats' patriotism for opposing the Civil War.

On the campaign trail, Republicans knew that to win the election they had to concentrate on getting the votes of northerners whose main concern was fear of the South. "Our strong ground is dread of a Solid South, rebel rule, etc." Hayes said in a letter to a well-known Republican. "I hope you will make these topics prominent in your speeches. It leads people away from 'hard times' which is our deadliest foe."

Republicans also unearthed the letter Hayes had written during the war saying he was so dedicated to the battle he would not leave the front to campaign for congressional office. Underneath the emotional speeches, however, Hayes was a moderate on the South. In his "Letter of Acceptance," he called for North-South harmony as long as the South accepted constitutional protections for blacks.

The South was the weak side of the Democratic platform. The Democrats hoped to distance themselves from the Civil War to win white votes in the South. At the same time, they did not want to irritate northerners' feelings about the war.

The Republicans did not worry about offending the South, since they could not hope to win the white southern vote by any means. Southern blacks would probably vote Republican anyway—if they voted freely. But the white southern Democrats were not about to let that happen. Across the South, they used terror and threats to keep the South's 700,000 eligible black voters from casting ballots for the Republicans. In the months before voting day, scores of blacks died in South Carolina in white riots meant to warn blacks against voting Republican. Many such clashes scared away blacks, who outnumbered the whites in some states. It was not to be a fair election, even before the charges of irregularity that would come out after election day.

Hayes was in Columbus on Tuesday, November 7—a cold, disagreeable day. That night he received reports of election returns showing that vote-rich New York had gone for Tilden. "From that time," he noted in his diary, "I never supposed there was a chance for Republican success." He went to bed after midnight, sure that he had lost.

Chapter 7

Election Tension

A t about 3:45 in the morning after election day, the *New York Times* received a telegram from a Democratic Party official: "PLEASE GIVE ME YOUR ESTIMATE OF ELECTORAL VOTES SECURED FOR TILDEN AT ONCE."

This request astounded the editors of the pro-Republican newspaper. They realized the election might be close, but if a top Democratic official could not figure out who had won, the outcome must really be uncertain. Managing editor John C. Reid, whose time in a Confederate prison during the war inspired in him a life-long hatred of Democrats, found the message especially intriguing. He wondered if it might not be useful.

Reid checked the figures and found that nothing final had come in from Louisiana, South Carolina, or Florida. The totals from other states showed that if these three states went for Hayes, the Republicans would win. Because all three states happened to have Republican Reconstruction governments, Republicans would be in charge of the official vote tally. Reid realized that if the local officials somehow made sure that these states went Republican, Hayes would be the winner.

Dashing over to the Fifth Avenue Hotel, Reid woke Republican campaign manager Chandler and explained his idea. "Go ahead and do what you think necessary," said Chandler, still half asleep. Reid and a Republican Party worker rushed to the telegraph office and sent a message to the governor of South Carolina: "HAYES IS ELECTED IF WE HAVE CARRIED SOUTH CAROLINA, FLORIDA, AND LOUISIANA. CAN YOU HOLD YOUR STATE? ANSWER IMMEDIATELY!"

Similar messages went to the other doubtful states. Soon replies came back, each stating that, indeed, these states all had been carried by Hayes. Chandler issued a public statement on the afternoon of the day after the election, declaring, "Hayes has 185 electoral votes and is elected."

To make sure the claim of victory came true, Chandler dispatched men to the South to pressure officials in key bodies called "Returning Boards" that certified the winner. This started a free-for-all of influence selling and bribery by Republicans and Democrats that snowballed into a total breakdown of political morality. Who really won? It soon became a choice between election by the violence of white organizations, or by money and deals under the table. Both forever clouded the results, leaving Republicans and Democrats alike with dirtied hands.

THE CANDIDATES

Tilden and Hayes, it was shown later, probably knew nothing about the fraud until too late. Tilden held a victory dinner at his home when early returns showed him sweeping to victory. Hayes was surprised to hear Chandler claiming victory. He told a reporter, "I think we are defeated despite the good news. I am of the opinion the Democrats have carried the country and elected Tilden." The next day the *New York Times* carried the headline: "The Battle Won: A Republican Victory in the Nation." This bold proclamation helped throw the election into turmoil. The newspaper reported the

Republicans had carried Florida, Louisiana, and South Carolina by good margins and gave specific vote totals. But in the days after the polls closed, headlines in other newspapers read, "Tilden Elected" and "Neck and Neck! Who Is It?" No one knew for sure who had won.

The Electoral System

When the votes were counted after the polls closed on November 7, it at first looked like a clear Democratic victory. Voters had cast about 250,000 more votes for Tilden. But under the American presidential election system, what count are not the votes of individual voters but those of electors, people appointed by the parties of each state to cast the state's electoral votes. Each state has as many electors as it has representatives and senators in Congress.

When a candidate wins the majority of the people's votes in a state, all the electors of that state normally cast their votes for that candidate. Thus, a win by one vote is as good as a win by a million; all of the state's electoral votes go to the winner. That means in close elections a candidate can come out with fewer votes from the people, but still win the election by amassing more electoral votes. This is what was happening when Chandler reported that Hayes had 185 electoral votes, one more than half of the total of 369.

After receiving the news of the election results in Columbus, Hayes continued to believe for days that he had lost. He went out to church and dinner on the Sunday after the election. When he returned home, he found Webb waiting excitedly with a message from a trusted Washington friend: ". . . YOU ARE UNDOUBTEDLY ELECTED NEXT PRESIDENT OF THE UNITED STATES. DESPERATE ATTEMPTS BEING MADE TO DEFEAT YOU IN LOUISIANA, SOUTH CAROLINA, AND FLORIDA, BUT THEY WILL NOT SUCCEED."

Hayes then realized that the presidential election was not settled after all. He became more hopeful and tried to maintain his composure. "We can regard the result with comparative indifference so far as our personal futures are concerned," he wrote. He said he would attend to his duties "as Washington would under similar circumstances."

Hayes wrote to William Smith on November 13. "I am of the habit, for a day or two past, of saying 'undoubtedly, a fair election in the South would have given the Republicans a large majority of the Electors, and also of the popular votes of the Nation; and I think that a fair canvass of the result will still give us 185 votes required to elect.' " President Grant ordered statesmen of both parties to look into the conduct of the election. Congress and the people watched and waited anxiously.

Republicans who ventured south to assess the situation, including Senator John Sherman, later reported to Hayes that the Republican victory was not the result of bribery and false claims. He questioned them extensively, satisfying himself that they were correct. "All concurred in saying in the strongest terms that the evidence and the law entitled the Republican ticket to the certificate of election," Hayes wrote in his diary. "I have no doubt that we are justly and legally entitled to the Presidency." But more was to be revealed later that would cast doubt on the election.

Thrown to Congress

Meeting a December 6 deadline, the Returning Boards reported to Washington officially, giving Hayes the crucial votes in Louisiana, South Carolina, and Florida. The Democrats immediately challenged the results. Democratic members of the boards, who held a minority position, reported their own tallies favoring Tilden. To add to the confusion, one vote from Oregon became clouded in a related dispute. The election now depended on which set of returns would be accepted. Under the Constitution, how the validity of votes should be determined was left unclear. Congress now had to decide.

As the Senate was then controlled by the Republicans and the House by the Democrats, Congress was deadlocked. The two Houses, after much arguing, agreed to leave the problem up to a specially established 15-member committee of five senators, five representatives, and five Supreme Court justices. The committee was divided between Republicans, Democrats, and independent justices of the Supreme Court. Hayes opposed the plan. The Democrats, with Tilden's passive approval, supported it.

To everyone's surprise, the fifth Supreme Court justice's seat, the one that held the balance in the carefully weighted committee, fell by chance to a loyal Republican, Associate Justice Joseph P. Bradley. This outraged the Democrats, but there was nothing they could do about it. Webb wired his father: " . . . BETS ARE 5 TO 1 THAT THE NEXT PRESIDENT WILL BE HAYES." Rutherford began planning his trip to Washington.

On February 1, 1877, the committee began reviewing thousands of pages of evidence showing much illegality. It would rule on the 22 disputed electoral votes, state by state. If only one of the questionable votes went to Tilden, Hayes would lose — and no one knew for sure how the committee would decide.

Fear of Rebellion

With every day that passed, the United States moved closer to the end of President Grant's term on March 4 without reaching agreement on who would replace him. Political turmoil, even revolution or military takeover, was feared should the deadline pass without the naming of a new President. Yet Congress haggled on, through February and into March.

Angry Tilden supporters urged their candidate to declare the people had been "robbed of their choice for president." He refused, saying it was an incentive to violence. To his and Hayes' credit, the candidates insisted on allowing the legal process to take its course.

Tilden forces, particularly in the North, had no such patience. Hot-headed rabblerousers called for civil war to claim the Democratic victory. In Indianapolis, a mass meeting was told, "millions of men" would "offer their lives for the sacredness of the ballot. . . . Whosoever has a sword let him gird it on." The Tilden supporters took up the slogan "Tilden or Blood" and promised as a last resort to muster a force of men and take up arms.

Threats such as these, some from the Republican side in defense of Hayes, contained an element of bluff, but no one could be sure. The country was abuzz with questions and rumors. If no President was chosen, what would happen? Would fighting break out? Might the military take over? Everyone remembered the war between North and South and the assassination of Lincoln. People shuddered to think of what might happen now.

Fear touched the Hayes home, too. For the first time in their lives, the mail included threats and warnings of danger. A bullet was fired through a window of their Columbus home while the family was at dinner. No one knows if this was an attempt on Hayes' life, but Webb took no chances. Armed with a pistol, he insisted on accompanying his father on evening walks.

THE DEAL

While the public focused on the political fireworks, men of power and wealth met behind the scenes. Hayes and his managers understood by early December of 1876 that the lega-

*Hayes is shown balancing the forces that gave him an uncom-
fortable presidential victory. The stick labeled "Returning
Boards" represents the dispute over votes. The bayonets sym-
bolize the government's troubled military presence in the South.*
(Library of Congress.)

cies of the Civil War, particularly economic questions, could
be bargaining chips for support in the congressional wran-
gling over electoral votes. They secretly arranged what would
become known to history as the "Compromise of 1877," a deal
that decided the dispute in Hayes' favor.

The compromise, however, decided more than who
would occupy the President's office. It "laid the political foun-

dation for reunion" of a nation still divided by the Civil War, as one historian wrote. It achieved this by exchanging violence as a means of settling differences for negotiation, by ending Reconstruction and recognizing a new political order in the South. This new order sacrificed the idealistic and humanitarian goals of the Civil War for economic and practical purposes.

"You Will Be President"

The idea of a compromise took root when an important southern newspaper editor paid a private call on Hayes. Colonel W.H. Roberts of the *New Orleans Times* sounded out Rutherford about the South. He said Hayes told him "that the carpetbag[ger] governments had not been successful; that the complaints of the southern people were just in this matter; that he should require absolute justice and fair play to the Negro, but that he was convinced this could be got best and most surely by trusting the honorable and influential southern whites." Roberts told Hayes that such a policy would win the support of southern leaders. "You will be President," he said.

In a long series of conferences, which Hayes' supporters conducted independently of their candidate, the deal was hammered out. It hinged on a basic fact about the Democrats: northern Democrats were spoiling for a fight over the election; they wanted to give up nothing. But southern Democrats, especially the former plantation owners and a new class of businessmen, hoped to avoid conflict. They had had enough of war and wanted more than anything subsidies—federal funds—to rebuild the devastated South.

The final version of the deal was set down February 26 at a meeting in Wormley's Hotel in Washington. The southern Democrats agreed to drop their support of a filibuster (a legislative talk marathon used as a delaying action) blocking the completion of the electoral vote count. That would permit Hayes to become President. In exchange, the South was promised aid for rebuilding and railway construction, a Cabinet seat, and a voice in doling out federal jobs in the South. Later, in exchange for promises that the constitutional voting and civil rights of blacks would be protected, the Republicans agreed to withdraw federal troops from South Carolina and Louisiana. This would effectively end Republican rule of southern state governments. It was the most controversial part of the agreement. Removing the troops would close what was left of the Reconstruction era. It would permit the whole South to be ruled by the whites, as it was before the war.

The deal was sealed and only the formalities remained.

President at 4:05 A.M.

Tilden stayed aloof from the political horse-trading, saying, "I prefer four years of Hayes' administration to four years of civil war." Had he been more aggressive, Tilden probably could have won the presidency. But he failed to act. Distracted by worries about his health, he let the Republicans take the initiative. Tilden would soon fade from the political scene.

The end of the drama came in the space of 15 minutes on March 2, 1877. At 3:55 A.M. the House doorkeeper announced the arrival of U.S. senators for a joint session of Congress. Temporary Senate President T.W. Ferry of Michigan led the party, closely followed by four men carrying revolvers. The armed guard carried two mahogany boxes containing the electoral returns from 38 states. As the senators took their seats, 10 more armed men took places at the front of the House chambers, posting themselves near the Speaker's chair, the ballot boxes, and Senator Ferry.

At this point, Congressman E. John Ellis of Louisiana shouted, "Democrats leave your seats!" About 60 lawmakers noisily walked out or to the back of the chamber. Another 30 Democrats stayed seated. The joint session continued.

Ferry stepped up to the rostrum to take his seat. Looking tired and nervous, he called for the reading of resolutions on the electoral count. The last 10 votes, those of Wisconsin, went to Rutherford B. Hayes and William A. Wheeler. At 4:05 A.M., Ferry declared: "This concludes the count of the 38 States of the Union." He then asked for the results from the clerk. A silence fell on the chamber as Ferry, shaking with emotion, put the final official signature on the document and said:

> Wherefore, I do declare: That Rutherford B. Hayes, of Ohio, having received a majority of the whole number of electoral votes, is duly elected President of the United States, commencing March 4, 1877.

He then announced Wheeler was duly elected Vice-President.

Someone shouted "shoot," startling the audience. But the only response was a faint hand-clapping by a newspaper editor friend of Hayes at the back of the chamber. No one else applauded. By 4:10 A.M. the session adjourned. The audience cleared out in three minutes. Ten minutes more and the lights were turned out.

Chapter 8

Lemonade Politics

When news of the final electoral count was received, the train carrying President-elect Rutherford B. Hayes chugged out of Harrisburg at dawn. When it reached Washington shortly after 9 A.M. on Friday, March 2, rain was falling heavily, but a crowd of 2,000 people had gathered to welcome Hayes. Senator Sherman met the train and escorted Hayes and Lucy to his carriage. They then drove to the senator's home.

Hayes purposely entered the capital as normally, openly, and as confidently as possible. Many friends advised him to enter Washington secretly for fear that he might be assassinated. But the idea of sneaking into town repelled him. His bold entry into the capital proclaimed that he had nothing to hide, nothing to be ashamed of, and that the nation was not in danger.

Senator Sherman met the train because Hayes had arranged to stay at Sherman's private residence before taking the oath of office. Grant had invited him to lodge at the White House, but Hayes declined, not wanting to appear overeager to move in. Hayes wanted to give no support to Democratic newspapers that were doing as much as they could to encourage doubt over his right to office. Headlines called him "His Fraudulency" and "Rutherfraud B. Hayes."

A CAREFUL BEGINNING

On February 28, Hayes had resigned as governor of Ohio and said goodbye at a reception in the state capitol. The next morning, he, Lucy, the children, friends, and political associates boarded two private cars on a Pennsylvania Railroad train at the station in Columbus. A railway magnate put the special cars at Hayes' service. Several thousand people cheered and a band played at the track-side send-off.

Hayes mounted the rear platform of the train, triggering cheers from the crowd. He beamed at the crowd's enthusiasm and gave a light-hearted talk. He remarked that "perhaps" he might "be back immediately." He talked seriously to the audience about the southern question. He said he had gone off to war in 1861 to help preserve the Union, "But there was something that force could not do. We would have our union to be a union of hearts, and we would have our Constitution obeyed, not merely because of force that compels obedience, but . . . because the people love the principles of the Constitution." This would be the theme of his speech at the inauguration.

Serving Party and Country

After his arrival in Washington, Hayes made courtesy calls on Congress and Grant. The next day he attended a feast in his honor at the White House. Grant, giving the last dinner party of his presidency, invited all the Washington bigwigs to attend. But as the guests drank to the new administration that night, shadows from the disputed election fell over the city.

Congress stayed in session that Saturday night. The still strong pro-Tilden Democrats passed legislation restricting presidential use of troops in the South. This was a message that Democrats and many Republicans would resist and attack Rutherford's presidency. Inside the White House, Grant was worried because scheduling of the swearing-in left the nation without a President between the expiration of Grant's term on Sunday, March 4, and the ceremony on Monday. This occurred because it was considered improper to hold an inauguration on Sunday, the Sabbath.

With so much talk of trouble, Grant wanted to take no chances. He called Hayes aside before dinner and asked him to go through with a secret oath-taking ceremony. Hayes reluctantly went along, joining Grant and Chief Justice Morrison R. Waite in the Red Room. He took the oath that he would take again publicly on Monday.

Because of the election dispute, the usual inaugural ball and inauguration-day parade had been canceled. Monday dawned cold and cloudy, but by midday the sky brightened. Hayes, wearing a black suit and black tie, stood on a platform draped with huge American flags. He took the oath of office and then addressed the crowd of 30,000 gathered for the ceremony. His commitment to clean up the civil service came through forcefully when he vowed that reform would be "thorough, radical and complete." Knowing this would ruffle the feathers of his party backers, he followed the pledge with a patriotic affirmation that was long remembered. He said, "He serves his party best who serves his country best."

The main thrust of the speech was devoted to the southern question. Hayes defended his position, saying to the South:

> It is my earnest desire to regard and promote their truest interests—of the white and colored people both and equally—and to put forth my best efforts in behalf of civil policy which will forever wipe out in our political affairs the color line and the distinction between North and South, to the end that we may have not merely a united North or a united South, but a united country.

The speech was a good one. As the crowds cheered, Hayes left to take up office in the White House.

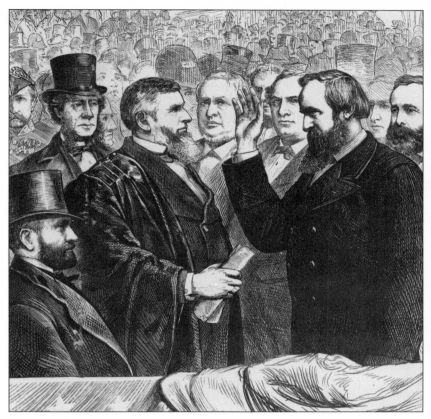

Chief Justice Morrison R. Waite of the U.S. Supreme Court administered the presidential oath of office to Hayes on Monday, March 5, 1877. It was the second time Hayes had taken the oath. President Grant held a secret swearing-in ceremony on Saturday for Hayes to make sure the nation had a President between the expiration of his term on Sunday, March 4, and the public ceremony. (Library of Congress.)

UNDER SIEGE

Rutherford's term proved to be one of much bitterness, infighting, and only a few political victories. There was little he could do to dispel the anger felt in Washington over his election. Even after four years in the White House and some major achievements, bad feelings persisted. One popular joke would be that "Mr. Hayes came in by a majority of one and goes out by unanimous consent."

But the warmth of the Hayes White House won many friends and admirers. Rutherford had a way with people. "Well, what do you know?" was his favorite greeting. He would remember the names and faces of people he had only met briefly years before. He put everyone at ease.

Lucy, in particular, helped overcome the hostility to her husband's presidency. She made the Hayes White House both a family home and a successful focus of Washington social life. As presidential hostess, Lucy arranged everything from state dinners to casual gatherings, welcoming guests and treating them with hospitality. She recruited Hayes' cousins, daughters of friends, and nieces to help host functions. They added a friendly, youthful touch to state dinners. Lucy became the first wife of a President to be regularly called "First Lady" of the White House.

During the early years of Hayes' term, Congress was so hostile that it refused to provide money for the upkeep of the White House. Lucy resorted to reversing the ends of curtains, covering worn spots in the carpets with furniture, and using other means to keep up appearances. She went through the attic for usable furniture and sometimes spent her own money to buy furnishings. Hayes voluntarily took on a portion of the cost of running the White House, spending some of the nearly $200,000 he earned during his term as President on White House needs. This was not hard for him because his inheritance from Sardis and wise investments probably made him the wealthiest President of the 19th century.

Despite harsh commentary on the Hayes presidency, journalists could not help but admire Rutherford and Lucy. "They don't look like usurpers, or people who would lend themselves to fraud of any kind," said a woman columnist. A reporter at the inauguration concluded, "Mr. and Mrs.

Lucy Webb Hayes and Rutherford in an 1877 portrait. (Library of Congress.)

Secretary of Interior Carl Schurz frequently played the piano for Hayes, his family, and friends at the White House. They would sing psalms together there regularly on Sundays. (Library of Congress.)

Hayes are the finest looking type of man and woman that I have ever seen take up their abode in the White House." She described Lucy's "gentle and winning face" under her black, straight hair.

On taking office at age 54, Hayes was in the prime of his life. He was broad-shouldered, five feet eight and one-half inches tall, but looked taller in his Prince Albert coat. His high forehead, dark-blue eyes, and full beard impressed his contemporaries. In the years of his presidency, his fair hair and sandy beard grew increasingly gray, and his weight increased from a hefty 180 to a paunchy 192 pounds.

Home Life

Behind the scenes, the Hayeses maintained their family life. Family members living at the White House included 21-year-old Webb, who served as his father's confidential secretary. Two other sons, Birchard, 23, and Rud, 18, lived away at college and visited regularly. Six-year-old Scott, and Fanny, then nine, were often included in White House activities. Sometimes they might be called out to meet the guests. Once, when Sioux Chief Red Cloud came to the White House to plead for his tribal lands, he patted Scott on the head and called him "young brave."

President and Mrs. Hayes encouraged friends to visit during informal gatherings often attended by noted artists, writers, and political leaders. At one such gathering, Thomas Edison demonstrated his recently invented phonograph. Sundays featured a regular psalm-singing time in the White House library, joined by Vice-President Wheeler. Secretary of the Interior Carl Schurz would accompany the singing on the piano.

Lemonade Lucy

Lucy, ironically, is remembered as the stern guardian against alcohol drinking in an overly thrifty White House. This reputation, which has remained in history books, grew out of the Hayes policy of not serving liquor at the White House. Liquor had not been served at the Hayes household in Ohio, and the family carried the custom to Washington. Rutherford, though not wholly opposed to drinking liquor, felt that a ban on liquor in the White House would set an example for the entire nation. The temperance movement cheered the decision; the press ridiculed it. Reporters apparently picked up a comment Hayes made about drinking lemonade, and later invented "Lemonade Lucy" as a nickname for Mrs. Hayes.

Not serving liquor led to the false assumption that the White House under Hayes pinched pennies on celebrations. On the contrary, Rutherford gave instructions to make up for the absence of wine at state functions with the finest decorations and entertainment available. His diplomatic receptions featured some of the longest expense lists of the time. The menu at a banquet might include gourmet servings of turtle, sweetbreads, meat patties, salads, ice cream and ices, cakes, coffee, lemonade, and sweetmeats. Flowers that Lucy grew in the White House conservatory brightened the rooms, and guests ate off elegant tableware decorated with paintings of nature scenes. These elegant dinners set a new standard for taste in Washington, and invitations to state dinners at the White House were in big demand.

A Place for Everyone

It can be truly said that the Hayes White House had a place for everyone in an easy-going spirit of accommodation. The family's hospitality strained the capacity of the White House.

At that time the offices of the President and his Cabinet were on the same floor as the living quarters, so officials and family shared corridors going to bedrooms and bathrooms (where running water was installed in the Hayes years). Rud claimed that when he and Birch came home from college, they seldom had a bedroom or even a bed to themselves. They might even be assigned a cot in the hall, a couch in the reception room, or even a bathtub as a "resting place."

At receptions for the public, Rutherford and Lucy stood in a receiving line for up to two hours shaking hands with everyone who came in. A thousand or more would pass through the line, until Lucy's white gloves lost shape and color. No one was ever turned away.

Hayes held public receptions that turned out to be costly affairs. Souvenir hunters stole crystal pendants from the chandeliers, cut pieces off the bottoms of curtains, and carried off anything else they could. Eventually, the open receptions had to be dropped, and after that it was by invitation only.

The now-famous annual White House Easter Egg Roll for children was started during the Hayes years. Lucy invited the children to the White House after Congress passed a measure forbidding the event on the Capitol lawn. She did not want to disappoint children who looked forward to the occasion.

Official Hayes

When he traveled outside Washington, Hayes tried to avoid pomp and formality. Sometimes, rather than order a special train, he would just buy a regular ticket and hop on the train. Usually no one recognized him without the presidential trappings and hovering officials. After one such trip to Baltimore, he met a "Mr. Sutton of Eastern Shore – clerk at the great wholesale store of Jacob & Co." Hayes said the man "took

Hayes, called "Rutherford the Rover" by his critics, spent much time traveling. On one of his first trips outside Washington, in June 1877, he and his family attended the annual reunion of the Union Army at a clambake in Providence, Rhode Island. (Library of Congress.)

a seat by my side. I got much interesting information about his business and the trade generally." This sort of exchange helped Hayes sound out public opinion.

On typical days, Hayes rose at 7:00 A.M. and wrote until breakfast at 8:30. Afterwards, the family gathered to hear the Lord's Prayer and a chapter from the Bible. He worked in his office until 10:00 A.M. writing all correspondence by hand. When he finished, he received congressional and Cabinet visitors until noon. Time was set aside for other visitors, particularly office- and favor-seekers, until 2:00 P.M., when he would eat lunch. He then went for a carriage ride from 3:30 to 5:00, napped, dressed for supper, and dined at 8:00. He greeted callers until about 11:00 and then took a short walk, accompanied by secret service guards, before going to bed.

The carriage ride after lunch was not just for digestion. In the Hayes White House, privacy was hard to find. Rutherford often conducted his most confidential business during the rides around Washington with associates and legislators. At times he hid in the bathroom to find the privacy he needed to prepare important state papers.

Chapter 9

Hyenas and Wolves

Despite angry Republican hyenas who had expected to wield influence behind the scenes, and in the face of assaults by Democratic wolves bent on obstructing or even toppling his administration, Hayes lost no time in unfolding his plans. Within days of taking office, he had performed his first official duty, the naming of a Cabinet—the council of men who would advise and help him run the federal government. He had begun considering names back in January. The choices he had made, with a few exceptions, reflected his determination to promote men on merit and fitness, rather than out of political obligation. They laid the foundation of Hayes' assault on the spoils system in federal government.

Rutherford's refusal to bend to political pressures pleased the public. However, it infuriated those Republicans who had expected to dictate Cabinet choices to the President. But Rutherford needed a strong, loyal Cabinet. Congress was in no mood for generosity, and two years into his presidency the Senate would fall to the Democrats, giving them control of both Houses.

AROUND THE TABLE

Every Tuesday and Friday the Cabinet officials would sit for two hours around the table in the President's high-ceilinged private office to discuss the weighty issues of government. Hayes' place was at the head of the table. Positions of the Cabinet members around the table marked their influence. To Hayes' right sat Secretary of the Treasury John Sherman, a thin, bearded man over six feet tall who managed the nation's economic affairs. To the President's left sat Secretary of State William M. Evarts, an outstanding New York lawyer who dealt with foreign relations. At the far end of the table, in a position of equal status, was Secretary of the Interior Carl Schurz, the first citizen of German birth to hold a Cabinet post. The colorful Schurz oversaw departments ranging from the Bureau of Indian Affairs to the Patent Office.

Men chosen for ability occupied most of the other positions, but a few appointments reflected political considerations. The Navy Department went to Richard W. Thompson, a choice designed to win the support of influential Republican Senator Oliver P. Morton. Unfortunately, Morton died within six months of Rutherford's taking office, causing a loss of political support from which Hayes never fully recovered.

A few appointments sent messages of sympathy to the South. For example, as postmaster general Hayes picked David M. Key, a southerner from Tennessee who was a Democrat and a former Confederate soldier. Key's appointment fulfilled the agreement by Hayes' supporters that he would name a southerner to the Cabinet. With the same goal in mind, Hayes later appointed a Kentuckian and former slaveowner, John Marshall Harlan, to the Supreme Court. This appointment proved to have a lasting importance because Harlan served on the court for 34 years and despite his background, championed black civil rights.

The Hayes Cabinet and his son, Webb, who served as the President's confidential secretary. From the left: Webb Hayes; the President; John Sherman, secretary of the treasury; R. W. Thompson, secretary of the Navy; Charles Devens, attorney general; William Evarts, secretary of state; Carl Schurz, secretary of the interior; George McCrary, secretary of war; and David M. Key, postmaster general. (Library of Congress.)

Hayes set an example for the South by appointing Frederick Douglass, a black man, as United States Marshall of the District of Columbia. This appointment "should be accepted as an indication of a purpose to advance equal rights of the people of the entire country," he told a delegation of black ministers.

TRYING FOR PEACE

On April 3, 1877, Hayes sent orders to Secretary of War George W. McCrary to return to "their previous place of encampment" the 19 enlisted men and two officers of the U.S. Infantry stationed at the state house in Columbia, South Carolina. On April 20, a similar message ordered federal troops back to barracks in Louisiana. These orders marked the formal ending of Reconstruction.

This act was partly symbolic. The number of occupation troops had already begun to dwindle in 1871. By the time Hayes took office, only two Reconstruction governments remained that were backed by federal forces.

The abandonment of military rule really originated with Hayes' predecessor, President Grant. Near the end of his term, Grant had ordered most of the troops protecting carpetbagger governments to return to barracks. At the time Hayes acted, just 3,380 soldiers out of the 25,000-strong U.S. Army protected Reconstruction governments. Because Congress had purposely failed to provide money to pay the occupation troops, Hayes would have had trouble keeping them in place even if he had wanted to.

Yet the official order removing the last troops held great political meaning. Hayes' new policy was called a "total departure from the principles, traditions, and wishes of the [Republican] party." It signaled an end to the policy of using force of any kind in the South.

Appeasing the South

For the Republican Party, Reconstruction had borne few fruits. Since the war, the South had turned mostly Democratic, depriving the Republicans of any regional political power except what they could maintain through the force of arms. With the northern public growing tired of keeping soldiers in the South, Hayes may have felt it was pointless to continue with military occupation. He felt the current arrangement had to change because he had come to believe, as most northerners did, that the carpetbagger governments were hopelessly corrupt and that blacks were ill-prepared for equality with the whites. Hayes wanted to end dependence on black voters to increase Republican strength in the South. Instead, he wanted to try to win power through cooperation with southern whites.

Removing federal troops eliminated the one element of Republican rule that white southerners objected to most. Hayes also tried to appeal to money interests in the South with offers of federal aid for "internal improvements," which southern businesses needed. And he appointed southern Democrats to federal jobs. All of these actions, he hoped, would lead to the formation of a new southern branch of the Republican Party. He thought southern white Republicans would support the rights of blacks in order to join with the North on economic issues that affected both sides.

By turning to whites for support, however, Hayes was in effect telling blacks to step aside and give up all political status they had gained during Reconstruction. He thought this loss would be temporary, that over time and with greater education the blacks could take back what they had lost. He believed they would be able to make use of legal means to protect their interests because white leaders promised him they would uphold the rights of both blacks and whites. Hayes wrote to his southern friend, Guy Bryan:

My theory of the Southern situation is this. Let the rights of the colored people be secured and the laws enforced only by the usual peaceful methods—by the action of the civil tribunals and wait for the healing influence of time and reflection to solve and remove the remaining difficulties.

Misplaced Trust

The summer after he took office, Hayes made a tour of the South to gauge the success of his policy. Because his sweep through the South met with cheering crowds, he felt his policy was "altogether happy and successful." There are "thousands of intelligent people in the South who are not Democrats and who would like to unite with Republicans of the North," he declared. But he was wrong.

The truth was revealed when, in the congressional elections of 1878, every southern state went overwhelmingly for white-supremacy Democrats. Incidents of racial violence, leaving 30 or 40 blacks dead in Louisiana, proved false Hayes' predictions of racial harmony. The Democrats used all available means to keep white and black Republicans from the polls.

"I am reluctantly forced to admit that the experiment was a failure," Hayes told a reporter. Privately, he admitted with some bitterness that, "By state legislation, by frauds, by intimidation, and by violence of the most atrocious character, colored citizens have been deprived of the right of suffrage—a right guaranteed by the Constitution, and to the protection of which the people of those states have been solemnly pledged."

Hayes had misjudged the South. Instead of responding to his overtures, whites clung to race prejudice, no matter how attractive the alternatives. They wanted, more than to find common interests with the wealthy classes of the North,

Office-seekers flooded into the White House almost from the moment Hayes took office. Here, they wait in the lobby for a chance to meet the President. Most went away disappointed. Hayes made few appointments and avoided giving out jobs as political favors. (Library of Congress.)

to avoid sharing power with blacks. Soon, the blacks would lose all positions they had gained in state and national governments. Hayes and other northern Republicans had not taken into account 250 years of racial bigotry that kept whites from accepting the rights of blacks. They failed to anticipate that lack of education and poverty would put blacks at a disadvantage in standing up for themselves.

At first, blacks had gone along with Hayes' plans to pull the troops out of the South, thinking it was only an experiment and that military rule could be re-established. They soon became disillusioned, however. Even black appointee Frederick Douglass accused Hayes of making a virture of his troop-removal policy when, in fact, it was motivated by political necessity. It was charged that Hayes had abandoned his anti-slavery principles in a move calculated to win the presidency. But Rutherford stuck to his program, convinced that the need to use force was over forever.

THE SPOILS SYSTEM

The amount of business handled by the government in the booming 1870s increased dramatically. Only near the end of the decade did the most basic forms of technology, such as telephones and typewriters, begin to ease the crush of office work. But at this time of greatest need, the spoils system, also called patronage, undermined the federal bureaucracy like a cancer. The system had worsened under the weak Grant and Johnson administrations, when positions of power tended increasingly to be occupied by men who earned favors by getting out the vote in elections.

Hayes tried to weaken the spoils system. He had the power under the system to appoint federal workers down to local postmasters. Upon being elected, Presidents before him would replace much of the federal workforce with members of their own party. But Rutherford limited himself mainly to filling vacancies and dismissing workers only for good reasons. He removed fewer federal employees than any President since John Quincy Adams and prohibited appointments of anyone related to him by blood or marriage. This meant that recommendations from congressmen, who had been used to rewarding supporters with federal jobs, now had less importance.

Hayes did not completely ignore the spoils system. He did make some appointments for political reasons in order to boost the party. He also made a few mistakes, which he later acknowledged, by appointing men of bad character. But overall, he worked to bring qualified people into government.

A key attack on the spoils system was the fight over control of appointments to federal jobs at the U.S. customhouse in New York City. Two-thirds of all imports to the United States entered through the port of New York. The revenues collected at the U.S. customhouse in New York City represented a major source of federal income. But the department was riddled with patronage appointments controlled by the New York political machine under Senator Conkling. More than 1,000 employees at the customhouse obtained their jobs for political reasons, and 20 percent of the workers were unnecessary. Corruption undermined the customhouse's every move.

Hayes wanted to replace the top men at the customhouse with people who had no political affiliations. But the Conkling forces in the U.S. Senate resisted. When Conkling rejected the people Hayes appointed as replacements at the customhouse, the first round of the fight went to Congress. (Senate approval is required for certain presidential appointments.) Hayes did not give up, however. When Congress adjourned in June of 1878, he used his powers to appoint when

CIVIL SERVICE REFORM.

IF YOU WANT GOOD WATCH-DOGS, YOU
MUST PAY A GOOD PRICE FOR THEM, AND
KEEP THEM WELL.

A HUNGRY DOG WILL STEAL.

IF YOU FIND ANY HONEST, CAPABLE, AND
FAITHFUL TO YOUR INTERESTS, DON'T TURN
THEM OUT TO STARVE WHEN THEY ARE
TOO OLD TO WORK.

*THE PRESENT SYSTEM WILL ONLY
PRODUCE CURS.*

*Uncle Sam is saddened by unchecked corruption in govern-
ment. Hayes fought for civil service reform, paving the way for
the modern civil service system put into practice years later.*
(Library of Congress.)

Congress was not in session to push out and replace the
Conkling men. Then, when Congress returned, Hayes
presented his appointees for confirmation and this time, by
exerting all his political influence, won approval.

"I have had a great success," Hayes wrote in his diary.
"No member of either House now attempts to dictate appointments. My sole right to make appointments is tacitly con-

ceded." It was the beginning of the end for the spoils system, and paved the way for the modern civil service system to take root in the 20th century.

Power of the Presidency

Hayes' victory over the spoils system was a milestone in boosting the power of the presidency. Despite his roots in the Whig Party, which advocated that the President only carry out the bidding of Congress, Rutherford worked to consolidate presidential power. He used his veto power 13 times, including seven vetoes in a row, to put down an attempt by the hostile Congress to railroad through legislation curbing presidential powers. Hayes moved the presidency back toward the more powerful form it had taken during the terms of Andrew Jackson and Lincoln, restoring for his successors many of the powers that had been taken by Congress during the Grant years.

This toughness won Hayes no friends in Washington. In early 1878, he wrote in his diary: "I am not liked as President, by the politicians in office, in the press, or in Congress." Things would briefly get worse before they improved. In the summer of 1878, the *New York Sun* revealed new evidence of fraud in the 1876–1877 presidential elections. This led to the opening of a congressional investigation into the disputed election by some Democrats and some disgruntled Republicans.

Led by Representative Clarkson N. Potter, the investigation succeeded in casting shadows on Sherman and other leading Republicans, but it quickly backfired. Instead of embarrassing Hayes, the Democrats unwittingly turned up evidence of massive Democratic wrongdoing. Republicans unearthed telegrams, many of them in secret code, between Tilden's nephew and contacts in the South. These were passed to the *New York Tribune,* which decoded and published them. One exchange went: "HAVE JUST RECEIVED A PROPO-SITION TO HAND OVER AT ANY HOUR REQUIRED TILDEN DECISION ON BOARD AND CERTIFICATE OF GOVERNOR FOR 200,000 [DOLLARS]." The reply: "DIS-PATCH HERE. PROPOSITION TOO HIGH."

This raised questions about how much Tilden knew of the telegrams, but the candidate denied any knowledge. The investigation revealed no evidence that he did know about them, even though many of the telegrams were addressed to his home. The public tended not to believe Tilden was so naive. The report dashed any hope for Tilden's political revival and muffled Democratic cries of fraud against Hayes. In defending the party against the charges that it had been a participant in the fraud, Republicans had actually come to the defense of Hayes himself. No wonder he considered the Potter investigation one of the "most fortunate" events of his administration.

Chapter 10

Of Telephones, Trains, and Travel

During the Hayes presidency, the United States was introduced to new habits of living: concrete sidewalks, iceboxes, linoleum floors, and mail order catalogs to name but a few innovations. Hayes would be the first President to put his ear to a telephone, when he heard the voice of Alexander Graham Bell from 13 miles away over a Western Union telegraph wire. Inventions like the automobile, the typewriter, the electric light bulb, and the phonograph would change everything. Railway travel became easier due to improvements by George Pullman.

In the economic recovery following the depression of 1873, ambitious men founded huge corporations that would come to dominate the nation's economy in the 20th century. The growth of big business spawned the labor union movement, bringing conflict with the working man, who was typically paid two dollars a day for 10 hours of work. Women also joined the workforce in growing numbers.

Massive immigration from central, eastern, and southern Europe crowded the cities. A squeezed urban humanity faced higher crime rates, dirty slums, and corruption-ridden political machines. At the same time, settlers poured over the Mississippi River into the western frontier, pushing out the Indians and building up new cities. Consumers discovered professional sports, ready-made clothes, and canned meats.

A fast-changing America was giving birth to the modern social and economic world. Hayes served as President at the dawning of this world, dealing with many of the growth pains these changes caused—and overlooking others.

BUILDING THE PRESIDENCY

Railroad workers had had all they could take. The business slump of recent years had steadily eroded their paychecks. Each time the amount of freight declined, the owners cut their wages while keeping managers' incomes steady and paying stockholders eight percent dividends. Brakemen were earning about $1.75 for a 12-hour day, and conductors received only $2.75. Work rules, such as a requirement that crews had to pay their own way back home at the end of a run, stretched the wages even more thinly. When, on July 16, 1877, managers cut another 10 percent from paychecks, railroad workers could stand no more.

Strikes and rioting broke out in Martinsburg, West Virginia, and spread like wildfire to Maryland, Pennsylvania, New York, Ohio, Kentucky, and Illinois. Rioters in Pittsburgh set a roundhouse on fire, destroying more than 125 locomotives and 2,000 freight cars. Police and state militiamen, poorly trained and outnumbered, fired at demonstrators out of panic, killing many people, including innocent bystanders. Governors in nine of 14 states hit by strikes sent urgent requests for federal troops to quell the rioting. It was the first labor outburst of national dimensions.

In 1876, while governor of Ohio, Hayes had been forced to use state militia to put down rioting sparked by labor disputes among coal miners. With this experience to help him, he proceeded cautiously in order to avoid the appearance of interfering in state affairs. He withheld help until governors formally requested it. In those cases where he decided troops were needed, Hayes ordered them in, and also issued a warning against further violence. He monitored the situation through telegraph messages, sometimes sent in secret codes, from military officers and trusted observers on the scene. The show of force helped end the rioting without further loss of life.

By sending troops, Hayes helped mold federal strike policy and moved away from an earlier hands-off tradition. Prior to that summer of 1877, the states and cities took sole responsibility for domestic peace. With Congress on vacation during the emergency, Hayes had taken the lead in dealing with the crisis. He set an example for later Presidents in cautiousness in the use of federal forces for domestic unrest and in the use of troops at times when Congress was not in session.

But Hayes' action helped restore peace without bringing the railroads and workingmen to the bargaining table. Though railway workers eventually received wage increases, the underlying causes of the strikes were left untouched. Hayes did not follow up on his actions with efforts to pass needed legislation. It was yet another decade before railway regulations were enacted, and even longer before laws were enacted to regulate labor.

Women Must Wait

Leaders of the women's movement hoped Lucy Rutherford's influence on her husband might advance their cause. Lucy, after all, was the first wife of a President to have received a college education. She was an inspiration to many women of her time. But evidently, she avoided using her relationship with Hayes to exert political influence.

A delegation from the National Woman's Suffrage Association went to the White House to appeal to Hayes to support laws that would allow women to vote. He met with them in the library, listened courteously, asked questions, and then promised to give their views his "sincere consideration." Before they left, he introduced the group to Lucy. Her comments to the women were not recorded. Apparently she sided with her husband on the question of women's right to vote.

Like many thoughtful people of the period, Hayes was willing to give certain privileges to women of special ability, but he believed most women had neither the ability nor the desire to vote responsibly. Popular medical literature of the time stated women needed all their energy to bear children and were too emotionally unstable to cope with serious matters. Women's suffrage would not be realized until half a century later. Hayes did, however, sign a bill in February 1879 allowing women lawyers to practice before the U.S. Supreme Court.

Greenbacks

Dollars then were either gold or silver coins or paper. Greenbacks were paper money that could be exchanged for gold or silver. But because there was no guarantee that the greenbacks would be redeemed for gold or silver, they were less valuable or stable than either precious metal. However, as a form of currency, greenbacks were simpler to issue.

In the economically troubled 1870s, businesses and farmers wanted the Treasury Department to print more greenbacks, hoping this would raise sagging prices and make it easier for them to repay loans. But Western mining states wanted the government to issue more silver money in order to boost demand for the metal. That would also push up sagging prices, it was believed. Generally, the Democrats favored greenbacks and silver while Republicans were divided on the issue.

Hayes, however, supported the "hard money" system of linking all dollars to gold—a traditional and widely trusted standard. This might not give immediate relief to people who had debts to repay, but he expected it to bolster the economy in the long run. Any other basis for money, he feared, could lead to a loss of faith in money's value, causing inflation— when prices rise too fast.

The battle mattered to westerners, who wanted easier credit. It mattered to easterners and foreign countries, who wanted stability in American currency. It mattered to people who had bought war bonds, which were loans made by individual citizens to the government during the Civil War. The financial system would affect how much money they would get on redeeming the bonds. The issue mattered to Hayes, who battled hard against two-thirds of Congress to win a victory against greenbacks. But his fight against silver money met with a stinging defeat and rebuke. Congress passed a law over his veto permitting limited coinage of silver as currency.

Oddly, by 1930, both gold and silver were dropped from the currency system. Paper money, "greenbacks," not convertible into precious metal became the standard. But events in following decades seem to bear out Hayes' concerns. Silver money failed to perform as hoped, but gold met expectations, helping to end the five-year depression in 1879.

After General Custer

For decades, the government had managed American Indians mainly with force, supporting the white man's push into the western frontier with troops of the U.S. Army and by mercilessly herding 300,000 natives into reservations. Hayes inherited this situation, taking office only days after "Custer's Last Stand," the defeat of U.S. Army forces under General George A. Custer by Sioux Indians. The battle marked a high point in the resistance of the Great Plains Indians to the white invasion. Hayes brought to the White House a measure of enlightenment that helped improve Indian-white relations.

Perhaps the most important decision Hayes personally made was to appoint Carl Schurz as Secretary of the Interior. This department administered Indian Affairs. But to enforce its decisions, it had to rely on the War Department, which wanted total control over the native Americans. Conflicts between the two left Indian Affairs in shambles and caused much injustice to the natives.

Schurz, backed by Hayes, led a successful battle in Washington to put the Indians fully under civilian administration of his department. He visited the Indian reservations and worked to end corruption, such as the cheating of Indians by government agents. Schurz fostered self-government for Indian tribes and promoted education, helping to do away with racist notions that the Indians were uncivilized and incapable of being civilized. Overall, Hayes' administration improved the rights and status of Indians. He counted "placing the Indians on the footing of citizens" among his successes as a President.

Quiet Abroad

Secretary of State William Evarts guided foreign policy. He inherited a well-organized and efficient department. Evarts' greatest contribution was to improve the consular service, the group of officials who worked overseas at consulates and embassies. He saw that these men could help increase the sale of American products abroad by sending back information useful to U.S. businessmen. This led to a push to gather commercial statistics that is today one of the consular service's most important activities. During Hayes' term, this led to a sharp rise in U.S. exports—the greatest Hayes legacy in foreign affairs.

No great foreign problems confronted the Hayes administration, but it did face three minor issues. Trouble cropped up with Mexico, where a new government took power in November of 1876. Hayes refused to recognize the new rulers until the Mexicans cracked down on Indian raiders crossing from Mexico into the United States. Mexico refused to cooperate until the United States dropped its practice of entering Mexico in "hot pursuit" of the raiders. Diplomacy to resolve the conflict failed, but over time, stability returned to Mexican affairs and the problem faded. Hayes then recognized the new leadership in Mexico.

Another problem occurred in Central America, when a French canal-building company attempted to begin the building of an interoceanic canal across Panama. Hayes considered this a threat to American dominance in the Western Hemisphere and eventually declared, "The policy of this country is a canal under American control." This declaration extended the "Monroe Doctrine," which was President James Monroe's message to Europe to keep out of political affairs in the Western Hemisphere. Hayes' defense of American rights in Panama extended the Monroe Doctrine to economic areas and laid the foundation for later U.S. policy in the region.

Relations with China were threatened during the Hayes years by outcries against Chinese laborers originally brought to the United States to help build the railroads. When the Chinese turned to other occupations, causing competition for jobs, many American workers protested. People demanded the government stop the influx of Chinese workers by breaking

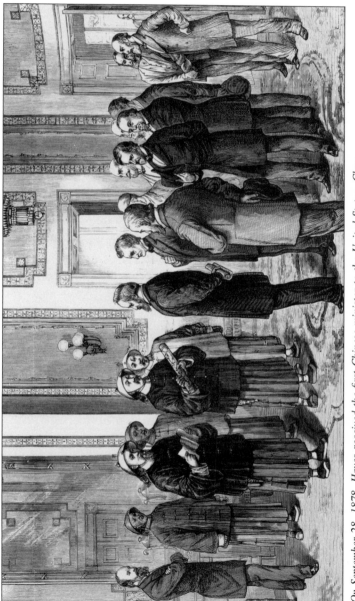

On September 28, 1878, Hayes received the first Chinese minister to the United States, Chen Lan Pin, in the Blue Room of the White House. This officially established diplomatic relations between the United States and China. (Library of Congress.)

a treaty with China that permitted unlimited immigration. Rather than break an international agreement and lose the trust of foreign countries, Hayes insisted on renegotiating the agreement with China. A delegation traveled to China, and an agreement was reached to "regulate, limit, or suspend the immigration of Chinese laborers" as needed by the United States.

GOING WEST

When Hayes traveled around the country, he told people of the need to live together in peace. He carried the message to New England and to the South. He spoke at soldiers' reunions and college graduations. He presided at museum dedications. But the most memorable way he conveyed the message was with a 72-day, 10,000-mile journey to the West in the fall of 1880. This trip not only showed that the United States was now one nation from coast to coast, it also allowed him to do something pleasant with the last few months of his term. And it gave him a chance to remove himself from center stage during the 1880 race for the presidency.

In making the trip, Hayes became the first President to cross the continent while in office. Traveling by train, steamboat, stagecoach, and army wagon, he and about 19 people, including Lucy and two of their sons, officials, friends, and a doctor, went from Ohio, through Chicago, across the plains and along the Pacific Coast up to Washington and Oregon. They then journeyed through the Southwest on the return home via Kansas City, St. Louis, and Hannibal, Missouri. At each stop, Hayes would make a brief speech praising the success of the American experiment.

While in Oregon, the group visited a government Indian school, where Hayes praised efforts to prepare the Indians through education to "become part of the great American family." Later, on their way to Santa Fe, New Mexico, the party had to cross through dangerous Apache territory. Under Army guard, they made the two-day trip rapidly, using fresh teams of horses stationed for them along the way by the Army.

A NEW PRESIDENT

"Superb weather, good health and no accidents," Hayes wrote in his diary after returning East. He reached Ohio on November 2, 1880, just in time to cast his vote for Republican presidential candidate James A. Garfield, who would succeed him as President.

Hayes ended his term on a high note, "enjoying one of the 'ups' of political life." In 1879 and 1880, an upsurge in the national economy brought better times to the country and credit to his economic policies. Even a usually critical newspaper was moved to refer to Hayes as a "remarkably cool hand; patient, wary, not capable of getting scared, a shrewd and long-headed politician." The 1880 election victory of the Republicans for the presidency and in Congress seemed to defy those who would brand Hayes' presidency as a fraud and a failure.

Hayes felt doubly pleased about his term in office when the Democratic Party pointedly passed up Tilden for nomination in 1880 and put forward Winfield S. Hancock, a man who had openly congratulated Hayes on his election in 1877. This helped Hayes end his presidency feeling "general content" with the results of his term. But few in his own time would praise Hayes' accomplishments. In general, commentary on his actions grew better in the years after he left office. History would concede even more. His presidency is now ranked by modern historians as being third in achievement among Republican Presidents, just after Lincoln and Theodore Roosevelt.

The week before the inauguration of Garfield, hundreds of Hayes' friends came to the White House to bid goodbye. Thomas Pendel, the chief doorkeeper, said that in his 36 years at the White House never had he seen more "weeping people" come to call.

Chapter 11
Going Home

After conducting President Garfield to the White House, Hayes and his family moved to John Sherman's home to spend their last night in Washington. On March 5, 1881, a Baltimore and Potomac train carried Hayes, his family, some friends, and a military escort toward Ohio and away from the "responsibility, the embarrassments, the heartbreaking sufferings" of life in the nation's capital. He and Lucy headed home eagerly, wishing "to get as completely back to private life as we can." Their joyous mood was soon severely jolted, however. As they neared Baltimore, the train engineer saw a passengerless train speeding toward them on the same track!

The engineer threw the engine into reverse, but not soon enough. The trains collided with a deafening crash! Hayes, riding in the fifth coach, was thrown from his seat. He was unhurt, but the crash left two others dead and 20 people injured. The engineer escaped with minor injuries.

This close call delayed the Hayes' return home for a few days, but the presidential party finally reached Fremont on March 8. A local band, a torchlight parade, banners, handshaking, and speeches greeted Hayes upon his arrival. He then described to the crowd what a 58-year-old former President should do as a private citizen:

Let him, like every good American citizen, be willing and prompt to bear his part in every useful work that will promote the welfare and the happiness of his family, his town, his state, and his country. With this disposition he will have work enough to do.

A QUIET FORCE

Hayes took his own advice, becoming one of the most involved former Presidents of all times. He appeared briefly in Washington after a disappointed and mentally deranged office-seeker shot President Garfield in the back on July 2, 1881. After Garfield died of his wounds on September 19, Hayes went to Washington for the funeral ceremonies and to escort Garfield's body back to Ohio. But most of the time he stayed out of the limelight in Fremont.

Hayes rejoined such local groups as the Odd Fellows (a men's public service club), and he became a member of a veterans' group and director of a new savings bank. He also helped raise funds for a local library. And although Hayes never joined a church, he would help out at Lucy's Methodist Church.

Hayes was still a force in society. He promoted education, serving as a trustee of universities in Ohio, and worked with a group for reform of prisons and criminals. He was especially interested in manual training, the concept that all children, rich and poor, should learn to use mechanical tools as well as their minds. He took leadership roles in such organizations as the John F. Slater Fund for Education of Negroes.

As far as the nation was concerned, however, Hayes quickly sank into obscurity. Winnie, the family's maidservant, found his retirement so lacking in excitement that she quit her job and went back to Washington to find another employer. Newspapers made fun of his obscurity, joking that he was not recognized at an unveiling ceremony at a monument and no one spoke to him—"except a policeman, and he told him to keep off the grass." In fact, however, Hayes was as active as ever but simply never sought attention. He just kept a public silence on political questions.

Retirement at Spiegel Grove

As the bright morning light filtered through the window at the Hayes' three-story mansion at Spiegel Grove, it would warm the library where Rutherford mulled over the day's knottiest problems and completed his most disagreeable tasks. Pen in hand, he would work at a desk in the corridor-like library. Books and memorabilia lined ceiling-high shelves on the facing walls.

At 8:00 A.M. Hayes would join the family at breakfast, returning afterwards to the library to deal with his pleasant correspondence. He would write letters to Civil War veterans, to a foundation working for the education of blacks, to reformers of criminals, and even to gossip columnists Lucy (who hated to write letters) had befriended in Washington. This would occupy the former President until about 11:00, when he stopped writing for the day. He would then go outside and walk at least six miles daily, perhaps more, before returning for lunch at 1:00 P.M. He would read and walk after lunch, but just around the house. Later in the afternoon, he would take carriage rides around Fremont, a town of 8,400 people, and then spend the evening with family and guests. This routine brought to Hayes the peace he had missed as President.

Lucy Dies

On a warm afternoon on June 22, 1889, Lucy sat in the bay window at Spiegel Grove, sewing. Her part-time secretary, Lucy Keeler, sat with her, reading descriptions of roses from a catalog. Lucy had wanted to order so many varieties that Keeler suggested jokingly that she list the flowers she did *not* want. When they finished, Keeler left and Lucy remained at the window with a servant, Ella, and both continued sewing. Outside, Scott, Fanny, and their friends played tennis.

The servant glanced at Lucy and suddenly became alarmed. She noticed that Lucy was "looking fixedly at her needle." Slumped in her chair, Lucy did not respond to Ella's questions. A doctor was called, and he diagnosed her illness as a stroke. Lucy was dying.

Rud was summoned from his job at the Fremont Savings Bank. Meeting his father at the train station later that day when Rutherford returned from a trip to Columbus, Rud told him how Lucy had been stricken. When Rutherford reached Lucy's side, she seemed to know him. "In her manner, she pressed my hand and tried to smile, or smiled!" Before too long, Lucy slipped into a coma. She died on June 25, just short of her 58th birthday.

Rutherford and Lucy had lived together happily for over 36 years. She was the "most interesting fact in his life," he used to say. On her death, he poured out his feelings into his diary, writing recollections of Lucy's beauty and character. He took special solace in the thought suggested to him by a niece that Lucy was in heaven with her first grandson, Ruddy, who had died as an infant in 1888.

Lucy's death brought Hayes closer to his own family and to his past. He visited Vermont to renew ties to relatives there, seeing a continuity of life that seemed to lighten his heart. He paused long at the graves of grandparents Rutherford and Chloe Smith Hayes.

Working for Change

In his quiet way, Hayes continued his life's work after Lucy's death. He believed in education as the only real solution to differences between races and ethnic groups. Once, when he visited a school for Indian children in Virginia, he condemned "sectionalism and race prejudice" as "the only two enemies America has cause to fear." He called for equality through education to fuse all "classes and populations" into "one great, harmonious whole."

Rutherford's involvement in the educational organizations enabled him to carry forward his ideas about education and racial conflict. One young black he personally helped was W.E.B. DuBois, who later became a leading spirit in the National Association for the Advancement of Colored People, a black organization that works to improve conditions for blacks in the United States. He also became more convinced of the justice of his southern policy when he toured the South in 1891 at the age of 69. He was received as a "friend of the South" and recorded that "Reaction, 'second sober thought' seems to be on my side."

During his retirement, Hayes watched the changes in industrial America and noted with dismay in his diary, the "rottenness of the present system." At the end of the 19th century, labor existed at the mercy of big money. Child labor and exploitation of women were common. The common working man became a virtual industrial slave, while managers and owners grew rich. The amassing of wealth, Hayes believed, allowed "a permanent aristocracy of inherited wealth to grow up in our country."

Hayes believed that big business should be supervised by government—which, in itself, is a very un-Republican idea. He went further. He spoke out against the concentration of property in the hands of the rich. These ideas would have been shocking to supporters of his conservative policies as

President. They went flatly against the stands of his former Whig Party. In his own day, such ideas would have allied him with "socialistic" and "communistic" views that horrified the upper classes. Hayes tried to find a word for the emerging concepts of "true equality of rights," finally deciding that, "The new tendency is 'a government of the rich, by the rich and for the rich.' The man who sees this and is opposed to it, I call a 'nihilist.'"

On to the End

On Sunday, January 8, 1893, Rutherford, at age 71, with snowy white hair and beard, rode in a sleigh to visit Lucy's grave. "My feeling was one of longing to be quietly resting in a grave by her side," he wrote in his diary. On Monday and Tuesday, he attended a meeting of the board of Ohio State University. The Democrats of the state, to Rutherford's delight, had named a building after him there. On this trip he interviewed a candidate for the post of director of manual training at the university.

After completing the interview, Hayes headed for the railroad station to take a train to Cleveland. A young university official, Alexis Cope, accompanied him, carrying his bag. "He [Hayes] took my arm and we walked to the station together. Arriving there, we found his train a half hour late. He proposed that we take a cup of coffee, so we climbed onto the high stools in the luncheon room and had our coffee." Cope thought Hayes "seemed nervously depressed and anxious for companionship." He talked of his early life, of his father's death, and of Sardis.

In Cleveland, Rutherford visited with his son Webb and a cousin. The next day he went about his business in Cleveland despite the deep snow and near zero temperatures. On

Saturday, January 14, Webb took Hayes to the station to catch a train to Fremont. They walked through the snow in the winter cold. Suddenly, Hayes felt severe chest pains. He sensed the end was near, but insisted on taking the train back to Spiegel Grove. "I would rather die at Spiegel Grove than to live anywhere else," he said. He managed to reach home, where, from his bed, he talked of new trips, of seeing Guy Bryan again in Texas. But he knew it was not to be. "I know I am going where Lucy is," he said.

Hayes died on January 17, 1893. He was laid to rest three days later on a clear, bright day. In a gesture honoring Hayes, President-elect Grover Cleveland, titular head of the Democratic Party, attended the funeral. His presence symbolically put an end to the bitter talk that Hayes had not been entitled to become President.

Bibliography

Barnard, Harry. *Rutherford B. Hayes and His America*. Indianapolis and New York: Russell and Russell, 1954. The most detailed and comprehensive biography of Hayes' life.

Davison, Kenneth, E. *The Presidency of Rutherford B. Hayes*. Westport, CT: Greenwood Press, 1975. A broad, thoughtful, and helpfully interpretive portrait of Hayes and his times.

Greer, Emily Apt. *First Lady: The Life of Lucy Webb Hayes*. Kent, Ohio: Kent State University Press, the Rutherford B. Hayes Presidential Center, 1984. Though the book focuses on Lucy Hayes, it provides an excellent glimpse of Rutherford Hayes' family life.

Hoogenboom, Ari. *The Presidency of Rutherford B. Hayes*. Lawrence, Kansas: University Press of Kansas, 1988. The most thorough and in-depth study to date of the presidential period.

Robinson, Lloyd. *The Stolen Election*. Garden City, NY: Doubleday & Company, 1968. A colorful account of the disputed election between Hayes and Tilden.

Williams, Harry T. *Hayes of the Twenty-Third*. New York: Alfred A. Knopf, 1965. A well-crafted portrait of Hayes as a Civil War soldier. Written in the context of military developments.

Index